D1758536

DUDLEY PUBLIC LIBRARIES

The loan of this book may be renewed if not required by other readers, by contacting the library from which it was borrowed.

STUART SURRIDGE

SKIPPER OF SURREY'S GOLDEN ERA

STUART SURRIDGE

SKIPPER OF SURREY'S GOLDEN ERA

JERRY LODGE

First published 2008

The History Press Ltd
The Mill, Brimscombe Port
Stroud, Gloucestershire, GL5 2QG
www.thehistorypress.co.uk

© Jerry Lodge, 2008

The right of Jerry Lodge to be identified as the Author
of this work has been asserted in accordance with the
Copyrights, Designs and Patents Act 1988.

British Library Cataloguing in Publication Data.
A catalogue record for this book is available from the British Library.

ISBN 978 0 7524 4773 5

Printed in Great Britain

Contents

Acknowledgements

Betty Surridge, widow of Walter Stuart Surridge; Stuart 'Tiger' Surridge, son of Walter Stuart Surridge; Brian de Neut; Peter Sparkes; John Surridge, son of Percy Surridge, brother of Walter Stuart Surridge; Battersea Library; Emanuel School; Minet Library, Lambeth; Local History Library, Southwark; Grays Library; Guildhall Library; Museum in Docklands; Roger Mann Photograph Collection; MCC Library – Glynis Williams and Ken Daldry; Nottinghamshire County Cricket Club Library – Peter Wynne Thomas; Surrey County Cricket Club Library; Surrey Statistics Group, particularly Brian Cowley and Michael Pearce;

Unless otherwise accredited, the photographs used in this book have been supplied by the Surrey CCC Photo Library and Archives and the private collections of Betty Surridge and the author. If any photographic source believes it holds the copyright of any photograph reproduced in this book, it should contact the publisher to rectify the matter

ONE

Early Years, Childhood and Interest in Cricket

Stuart Surridge holds a unique record in the history of English cricket. Appointed to the captaincy of Surrey County Cricket Club at the age of thirty-four, he led his team to win the County Championship in each season under his guidance between 1952 and 1956. It is an even more remarkable story still, since while it took place in the days when an amateur cricketer was asked to captain a county side, it was unusual for a player nearing the end of his career to take on the role, particularly as Surridge was running a successful business with his brother from their head office in the Borough, some three miles from the Oval. He is now acknowledged to be one of the most successful county captains of all time and, in 1952, part of perhaps the greatest county side ever. After his retirement, the team went on to win the Championship for a further two years under the captaincy of Peter May

In the years immediately after the Second World War there were signs that Surrey would have a useful team, although it was recognised that they had a weakness in their batting. Under the captaincy of Michael Barton they shared the Championship with Lancashire in 1950 but dropped to sixth in 1951. The time was ripe for a forceful captain to bring the team to fulfilment; Surridge was the person to accomplish this feat. It can be argued that the captain of a cricket team can influence the performance of his colleagues to a degree higher than the captain in any other team sport.

Plaque on pavilion wall.

P. Stuart Surridge in 1911.

The Surridge family has had connections with Surrey for over a century and Stuart's grandfather founded the family firm of sports goods manufacturers, which continues to this day under the name of Surridge Sports, although the family no longer have any financial involvement in the firm.

As both visitors and Surrey members enter the Oval through the Hobbs Gates, they approach the pavilion where they find a plaque on the wall commemorating the performance of the 1952 team under Surridge's captaincy. It was a fine achievement for the county and established the leadership of Surridge, a popular leader in any case, and set Surrey on the road to further success.

Entering the pavilion, there is a large painting on the wall featuring the players and members in 1911 and one of those members is Stuart Surridge's grandfather. Born on 3 September 1917 at Herne Hill, London, Walter Stuart Surridge was fortunate to have a father closely connected with the game and one who could afford to give him the utmost encouragement. In 1921, his father bought the house at Earlsfield

Road, Wandsworth, which was close to Emanuel School, where Stuart and his older brother, Percy were educated. An advertisement in the local paper in March 1933 stated that Emanuel School could provide a public school education with all the requisite facilities at the school on Wandsworth Common. Set in grounds totalling twelve acres, it also provided excellent sporting facilities both there and at Blagdons, Raynes Park. The latter premises continues to be the sports ground for Old Emanuel to this day. The fees for the school in 1933 were £7 7s per term, with a reduction for brothers.

Stuart evinced a very early interest in cricket and at the age of eight took part in matches at school. The only member of his family to take seriously to the active side of the game, he progressed through the Under-14 team and the Colts to the First XI, which he captained in 1935, during his final season at the school, without achieving special prominence. As detailed in *Wisden*, he played 16 innings in 1934 scoring 255 runs at 17.00, with a highest score of 77, and took 17 wickets at 25.17. The School XI beat the Young Players of Surrey, scoring 121 against 115. In the match against the Parents he took 5-26. In 1935 he played 11 innings, scoring 173 runs at 15.72 and took 29 wickets at 13.75. Until his final two years at Emanuel he kept wicket, a fact which may well account for the alertness he subsequently showed in the field. He became a fast bowler by force of circumstance when, as he put it, 'The school hadn't a fast bowler, so I took on the job.' That statement typifies the man.

Trawling through his reports in the Emanuel School Library it is noticeable that his approach to his academic studies was poor. The headmaster, C.G.M. Broom, wrote in 1933: 'Disappointing, his standard of work is deplorably low.' And then in the Christmas 1934 report he stated: 'An admirable footballer. I shall like to see his reports recording some proof of his practical intelligence.' Reading in the school magazine there are the following comments on his activities at sport. For the rugby season of 1934/35 he was reviewed as 'a good all-round forward who has plenty of dash in the open and has often shown good judgement in making use of unexpected opportunities'. In the 1935 *Cricket Notes* the review said: 'A very successful season led by W.S. Surridge. An excellent captain who has devoted considerable

Emanuel School First XI, 1935. Stuart Surridge, middle row, second from left, next to the headmaster. (C.G.M. Broom)

time to training the team and has done it well. A batsman with a wide variety of scoring strokes and a useful fast bowler.' It is no surprise that Stuart was appointed as a prefect. This was the first official sign of his latent leadership qualities.

Emanuel did not employ a coach but as a schoolboy member of the county club from the age of twelve, Surridge attended the Easter classes at the Oval supervised by Alan Peach, and during the winter months improved his cricket at the indoor school in Wandsworth, then run by Andy Sandham and Alf Gover. For his advance as a bowler he owed much to Gover, for so long the spearhead of the Surrey attack, which helped enormously to correct faults in his action.

Alan Peach played for Surrey as a more than useful all-rounder from 1919 to 1931. He also played Minor Counties cricket for Berkshire in 1933 and 1934 and returned to Surrey as a coach from 1935 to 1939 where he took particular interest in the Young Players of Surrey side. This team was equivalent to a 'Colts' side for developing the talents of possible future professionals. Stuart Surridge was always an 'amateur' but played in this team and not for the 'Young Amateurs of Surrey' which consisted of players who enjoyed club cricket and had lesser ambitions of playing county cricket.

Alf Gover was the leading fast bowler in the Surrey side from his debut in 1928 until 1947. In 1938 he took over Herbert Strudwick's share of a cricket school in a partnership with Andy Sandham that was located on East Hill in Wandsworth and which was in walking distance of the Surridge home. After the war, he bought out his partner and spent the next forty-four years there as a coach. The school gained a worldwide reputation and players of all abilities from novices to Test stars used the facilities and valued his technical knowledge. Alf Gover became a particular friend and mentor of Stuart Surridge.

Stuart's life reached a crossroad when he left school at the age of seventeen. His father, silver-haired, neatly dressed and a well-known figure at most cricket grounds, urged him to go to Oxford to develop his cricket. The opportunity was there for the taking, but young Surridge, knowing of his poor academic record, and who had inherited much of his father's forceful personality, preferred to get straight down to work in the family firm. At his father's insistence, he started at the bottom in the business by simply becoming one of the workforce. He lived with his new colleagues in their little cottages and worked alongside them, which gave him useful experience in appreciating the attitudes and customs of professional artisans – characteristics that he may not have had the opportunity of learning – or understanding, from the confines of the company head office. It was a further example of how Surridge developed his excellent man-management skills.

For the next four cricket seasons he played for Old Emanuel with very good results. In 1936 he scored his first century, 106 *v.* West Surrey, and took 9-30 in the match against the school. In 1937 he bowled over 400 overs, taking 108 wickets at 11.36. In the match against Parsons Green, the Old Boys scored 181 and then bowled out their opponents for 12 with Surridge taking seven wickets for just seven runs.

The following year he again bowled over 400 overs and took 118 wickets at 10.68. His highest score with the bat was 68. The 1939 season was shortened owing to the start of the Second World War but he still managed 81 wickets at 13.40.

TWO

Family
and Start of Business

Percy Stuart Surridge, the grandfather of Stuart Surridge, was born on 27 August 1857 at Leigh-on-Sea, Essex. He married Clara from Plymouth and they had seven children: Clara Ethel, Percival, Frederick, Lilian Maud, Beatrice, Elsie and Gracie. His eldest son was named Percival, a tradition which has passed down through all generations of the family. By 1881 the family was living at 112 Rockingham Street, Newington, London, where Percival, the father of Stuart Surridge, was born on 23 May 1887.

Grandfather Surridge worked for Lillywhite Frowd in Regent Street and, being a carpenter, built most of the display cabinets on the shop premises, many of which have survived to the present day. He was such a skilled craftsman in wood that he also made violins. He was introduced to the craft of making cricket bats by James Lillywhite, but which James Lillywhite is not certain.

According to Hugh Barty-King in his book *Quilt Winders and Pod Shavers* the Lillywhite boys were a confusing bunch and needed sorting out. Was the James Lillywhite, manufacturer, of 3 Queen's Circus, Cheltenham, who was advertising in James Lillywhite's *Cricketers Annual* of the 1870s, the James Lillywhite who was the cricket coach to the public school in that town, and the eldest son of the famous Sussex cricketer William 'Non Pareil' Lillywhite? And did he have Stuart Surridge as an apprentice? This James's brother Fred had gone into partnership with John Wisden in 1855 in the London 'depot' and when this was dissolved in 1858, according to Alison Adburgham, he set up a cricket bat-making business with his brother John, William's second son, who was also a public school cricket coach at Rugby and Harrow. This was the firm trading as John Lillywhite from 10 Seymour Street, Euston Square, who exhibited 'articles connected with cricket' in the International Exhibition, held in London in 1862. In the same year, John Lillywhite filed a patent for a bowling apparatus in conjunction with Thomas Nixon, the inventor of the cane handle for cricket bats.

Surridge's master may, on the other hand, have been James Lillywhite, junior, cousin of the previously mentioned James. This Lillywhite was a member of Willsher's team which visited North America in 1868 and, in 1877, managed the first ever Test match, captaining the England side against Australia. The workshop of James Lillywhite, Frowd & Co. had been at Newington Causeway since 1863. Here they stored and seasoned well-oiled cricket bats in a 50ft-long warehouse, and in winter kept them at a high temperature to bring them to first-class condition for the following season and 'fit them for export to the hottest climates'.

Percy Surridge designed a refinement to the cricket bat by adding a reinforced toe and suggested that Lillywhite incorporate this design into their bats. The offer was declined, so Surridge took out a patent on the idea and started making bats in his shed at the family home in Rockingham Street. This was the start of the Stuart Surridge business in 1893 and advertisements for the original Surridge bats appeared in the Lillywhite Frowd yearbooks at some time around 1900.

He set up a workshop at 175 Borough High Street, London, SE1, close to the factory of James Lillywhite, Frowd & Co. at about the same time the Surridge family moved to a new home at 19 Amesbury Avenue, Streatham, as detailed in the 1901 census. He became a member of Surrey County Cricket Club in 1897 aged forty, and remained so until his death in 1919 at the age of sixty-two.

In 1902 Percival Surridge purchased the property known as 'Hillside', residing at 149 Atkins Road, Clapham Park, from the Trustees of the will of William Frankish. The site consisted of a house and garden on a plot measuring 150ft by 350ft for which he paid £1,500. This was on the Clapham Park Estate that had been created by Thomas Cubitt, the nineteenth-century builder responsible for London's Belgravia, Queen

Victoria's Osborne House on the Isle of Wight and the enlargement of Buckingham Palace. He chose Clapham for his home and as the place to experiment with a new housing development for rich clientele.

The estate was developed between 1825 and the 1860s, consisting of mansions and villas, each within spacious grounds, set alongside wide, tree-lined roads. These roads are now known as Poynders Road, Atkins Road, Thornton Road, New Park Road, Weir Road, Clarence Avenue and Kings Avenue. In 1825 he leased 229 acres in Clapham from the Lords of the Manor, the Atkins-Bowyer family. This land, lying to the south and east of the already-fashionable Clapham Common, included the standing buildings of Bleak Hall Farm. To provide good communication from his new estate, Cubitt bought several other small pieces of land to improve the roads that linked Clapham Park to the main London and Brighton roads, like the winding Dragmore Lane connecting Clapham Park to the common, which became Cavendish Road.

The plots in Clapham Park were laid out for detached villas standing in grounds of between half an acre and three acres, usually with stabling attached, and for larger mansions set within larger grounds. Since the land was very barren, Cubitt embarked on an ambitious scheme to enhance his 'garden suburb' by planting trees and shrubs. It was a shrewd investment since Clapham Park came to be admired for its quiet and verdant aspect. 'The foliage and the trees so luxuriant that during the summer months not a house is visible' was how a residence in Clapham Park was described in 1876.

Upwards of a hundred properties had been built in Clapham Park by the 1860s. Unlike later garden suburbs, Cubitt did not equip Clapham Park with pubs or other public buildings, perhaps feeling that residents would naturally embrace the rich social life already existing in Clapham.

Some suburban detached and semi-detached houses also went up in the 1930s, particularly in the area around Clarence Avenue, Atkins Road and Thornton Road. Most twentieth-century building in Clapham, though, has been put up by the local authorities including the London County Council, its successor the Greater London Council, Wandsworth Borough Council, and, after 1965, Lambeth Borough Council. When Cubitt's Clapham Park villas came tumbling down, the local authority's Clapham Park Estate went up (the boundaries do not correspond with Cubitt's estate). Building started around the Atkins/ New Park Road (Clapham Park East) junction in the late 1920s and continued until the 1970s.

By 1913 the Surridge family had moved into Hillside, the house and workshop standing in an acre and a half of grounds. 'His bat making is carried on with a very picturesque setting,' stated a report in *The Sportsman*, 'as there are no less than 130 fruit trees in the garden and sixty recently planted willows.' When the writer of the article visited Surridge's works he found the well-known 'Razor' Smith, the Surrey professional, hard at work with a 'Beetle', a heavy wooden mallet. It was duly recorded that:

The swinging of this instrument requires considerable strength and is perhaps as fine an exercise as one could have. Smith, who for seven years did practically no manual labour in the winter, finds this hard work beneficial, and has most satisfactory results so far as fitness is concerned. Last season [1910], it no doubt helped him to top the English bowling figures.

After Surridge had axed his willows at Clapham Park and put them through a planing and spindle machine and left them to mature, he sent them to his Borough workshop for modelling and finishing. 'The young princes Albert and Edward Prince of Wales may rest satisfied that the bats that he has supplied them with were fashioned in the most congenial surroundings of any manufactory.' Apart from the royal brothers, Surridge counted among his customers the cream of the aristocratic amateurs of this golden age of cricket: Lord Hawke, Lord Dalmeny and the rest, and 'many cases of his famous bats have found their way to the Rajah of Patiala and the Jam Sahib of Nawanager, the well-known 'Ranji'.

British cricket bat makers revelled in the situation which gave them a worldwide monopoly of a craft which 'the Dominions' had not yet acquired. With an increasing demand for English cricket bats coming from Australia, New Zealand, India and South Africa, cricket bat manufacture for home and overseas markets became an industry in the fullest sense of the word. Exporters like Surridge tended to congregate in the capital where the transport facilities were located close to the London Docks.

Since last November [1909] Mr Stuart Surridge has felled between 500 and 600 trees, all of the close-barked variety. He still retains over a hundred ready for cutting, and always realising the value of the best material, Mr Surridge has made arrangements for a continual supply to carry him over many seasons. The largest willow tree which has ever come under this popular maker's notice was grown at Robertsbridge in Sussex. Its circumference actually measured 21 ft., and from this over a thousand bats have been produced. Cricketers are invited, and will do well to pay a visit to Mr Surridge's yard in the Atkins Road, Clapham Park, where without doubt the finest selection of clefts may be selected from. Here there are stacked some 25,000 bats in the making, undergoing the process of seasoning, as the bat is ready for use under thirteen months from the date of felling the trees.

The secret of Mr Stuart Surridge's success has been his unrivalled knowledge of willow and his foresight in never allowing himself to run short of the raw unseasoned material.

Up to the 1850s, run-of-the-mill bats were mostly made of willow, either one hunk of wood carved into the shape of a bat, or a willow blade spliced into a willow or ash handle, at first solid and then made springy and resilient with whalebone strips. But in 1853 a craftsman-cricketer called Thomas Nixon conceived the idea of making the handle springy, not by inserting springs in a naturally unbending handle, but constructing the handle of a wood which was itself springy; he chose cane.

It is fascinating to consider why the cricket bat industry was so strong in England. Bats were, and still are, made from willow and the best bats come from one specific willow known as *salix alba*. Willow grows particularly well close to watercourses and although grown in various parts of England, a great proportion of the best timber for the cricket bat industry comes from East Anglia. Willow is not only extremely resilient and tough, but light. It is naturally soft, and herein lays the secret of its strength. Hardness is added mechanically. Types of willow other than the *salix alba* were not thought to have the fibrous tenacity for bat making. Many attempts have been made to grow willow trees in other cricketing countries but have not been able to achieve the quality of English willow. Some 10,000 English trees were needed for the cricket bat industry each year with thirty to forty clefts being taken from each tree. Willow is exported to India, Pakistan, South Africa and Australia.

In 1878 the number of cricket bat makers in London, encouraged no doubt by the reception given to Nixon's cane-handle invention and the boost it gave to the trade, swelled to twenty. By 1913 the business premises of the company had moved to 210-212 Borough High Street, London SE1 and Vine Yard, Marshalsea Road, London SE1. In 1915, Stuart Surridge & Co. Ltd was registered as a public company, the directors being Percival Surridge Sr and Percival Surridge Jr. During the First World War, the factory premises were converted for war production and, among others, the Surridge daughter Beatrice made leather belts and leggings for the army on the machinery in the workshops that had been designed for making cricket pads. She was also a driver with FANY (the First Aid Nursing Yeaomanry), much to her father's disgust.

In 1930, Hillside was sold to London County Council under a County of London (WA) Housing Order for £5,500. Percival Surridge's address at that time being Russell Hill, Purley, Surrey. His son, Percival Surridge married Edith Alice Clarkson on 30 August 1913 and they had three children Percy, Walter Stuart and Lorna. At the time of their marriage they were living at Hillside, but by 1917 had moved to 29 Milton Road, Herne Hill, where Walter Stuart was born. Percival was a member of Surrey County Cricket Club from 1921 at the age of thirty-four until 1951, aged sixty-four. From 1948 to his death in 1951 he was on the Surrey committee. In 1921 they had moved to 28 Earlsfield Road, Wandsworth.

By 1938 the business premises in the Borough had an additional site in Revesby Street. Apart from being sports goods manufacturers, they were listed as contractors to the Admiralty, the Royal Air Force, War Office and London County Council. Besides being a director in the family business, Surridge maintained an interest in two farms at Horley in Surrey and Aldermaston in Berkshire, where willow trees were grown from which cricket bats were made and sold.

In 1939 the directors of the company were listed as Frederick Walter Surridge, haulage contractor, of 136 Roehampton Vale and Percival Clarkson Surridge, sports goods manufacturer, of 28 Earlsfield Road. By the time of his death in 1951, Percival was running the business without involvement from Frederick and the business then passed to his sons, Percy and Walter Stuart Surridge.

Frederick Surridge, 'The Golden Dustman', and the uncle of Stuart Surridge, was born in 1890. He married Lily Mansfield and had two children, Peggy and Freda. He died in 1950 at the age of sixty. He was a member of Surrey County Cricket Club from 1921 aged thirty-one until his death. Both Frederick and his brother Percival served in Surrey Yeomanry Territorials before the First World War. One of their friends was a Mr Clarkson whose sister married Percival Surridge, Stuart's father. At this time, they applied for a contract with Wandsworth Council for the collection of rubbish. When duly awarded the contract, they borrowed £500 from their father and named the company after him. His father objected and the name of the company was changed to F.W. Surridge. It would appear that this may have been a joint venture between Percival and Frederick but later it becomes apparent that Frederick was the driving force behind the refuse removal company.

Frederick Surridge obtained the contract for clearing the dustbins in Wandsworth with his horse and cart. Then he happened upon the contract for removing the spoil that was excavated during the construction of the London Underground. Owing to the proliferation of work, the refuse collecting business grew quickly, allowing carts and carts of spoil to be transported to Essex, where Surridge started planting willow trees. And from the willow trees grew the bat industry.

The rubbish was collected from the streets by horse and carts and then moved by barge up the River Thames to a land reclamation site at Mucking, Essex. Frederick bought wharfs at Wandsworth in Rafts Road and Crown Cottage at Mucking. The wharf at Mucking was purchased along with an adjacent farm which by 1936 was a model farm, committed to traditional methods of husbandry, and one of the first to introduce electric milking machines. Not surprisingly, Frederick Surridge became known as the 'Golden Dustman'.

In 1933, as reported in the *Wandsworth Borough News*, Essex County Council attempted to present a Bill in Parliament to have the site at Mucking closed, as the rubbish was dumped in layers and then protected by a foot of earth. The councils of Finsbury, Hammersmith and Lambeth agreed to side with Wandsworth in opposing the plans of Essex County Council and were obviously successful for the Mucking site is still in use. Fred Surridge had extended his business to other London boroughs, which we can assume were those supporting Wandsworth in their fight with Essex County Council. From the same source, it is established that motorised dust-carts were introduced in Wandsworth in the early 1930s and the use of shire horses were phased out before the Second World War. At some stage, F.W. Surridge became Metropolitan Cartage Co. and by 1950 he had premises at 56 Nine Elms Lane, London SW8.

The Great Lakes Farm at Horley was bought by Grandfather Surridge in 1919 as a rest home for the shire horses used on the dust collection carts in South London, as well as being used to breed shire horses. The horses had been walked back and forth to South London. It was a mixed farm with both dairy and crops such as wheat and barley. When the milk quota was lost, the farm became run down and, currently, is not being used. There is the possibility of redevelopment into housing, subject to the usual planning restrictions.

THREE

Pre-War Cricket for Surrey

Surridge played for Emanuel School against Young Players of Surrey in 1934. Emanuel won by six runs in a match where Surridge probably kept wicket and scored 30 runs before being caught by Pierpoint off the bowling of Arthur McIntyre.

On leaving school after the 1935 season, Stuart Surridge became part of the Young Players of Surrey side in 1936. Eric Bedser recalled in the Surrey Yearbook of 1988 that:

Time does not so much fly as gallop, and it is hard for my brother Alec and I to realise that we have been firm friends of Stuart Surridge for fifty-four years… since we first met and played together for the Young Surrey Players, a collection of apprentices cutting their teeth against high-class club teams. Under the guidance of county coach Alan Peach, who was almost our personal guru, the young pros on the staff, reinforced by promising club cricketers in their teens, were first put to the test.

Apart from Stuart there was Arthur McIntyre, Geoff Whittaker and Bernie Constable. Add Alec and me and there were no fewer than six of a future Surrey side which carried all before it. And two internationals – not a bad investment, and a lasting memorial to the influence of Alan Peach, who, by good fortune, was a close friend of Percy Surridge, Stuart's father.

Father Percy was stern but kindly, and did not believe in spoiling his sons. Alan Peach was the son of a gamekeeper, who helped to look after the Surridge farm at Aldermaston, and no doubt, was influential in stimulating Stuart's great interest in shooting. Now shooting is his main sport, and he is an excellent shot.

In those happy pre-war days Stuart made a notable contribution to the side by being the only member whose father owned a car! It was a large Buick and he used to cram six to eight of us into the protesting vehicle to take us to some of the out matches. Since we had otherwise to carry our bags on to buses and trains and walk the rest of the way to the ground, to arrive in style was a treat especially as our generous chauffeur seemed to regard his duties as a privilege.

Though we could hardly have known at the time, the Young Players of that Surrey team, which kept together until the start of Hitler's War, were forging the nucleus of the skill and spirit of the Surrey of the Surridge years. The togetherness of the dressing room was comfortably re-established and maintained after the war; indeed we carried on as if there had been no gap of six years.

In his eight matches in 1936 Surridge scored 176 runs at an average of 22.00 with a highest score of 54 against Roehampton and he was the top scorer coming in at no.8. He bowled 84.2 overs in these matches taking 12 wickets at 22.50, his best performance being 5-94 against Surrey Club & Ground at the Oval, where one of his victims was Nigel Bennett, destined to be the Surrey captain in 1946.

In 1937 Surridge had three matches in the Second XI and although given little opportunity of performing with the bat, he returned one good performance with the ball, taking 5-19 in the first innings as Surrey beat Kent at Folkestone. There were two further matches for the Club & Ground in which his father also played three innings of 49, 10 and 4. But the majority of his Surrey cricket was still for the Young Players, where in eleven matches he scored 185 runs at 18.50 and took 20 wickets at 15.20. The team was very successful, winning most of their matches and Surridge had one outstanding bowling performance of 5-17 against Cranleigh. He scored one half century – 57 against Merstham.

By 1938 he had become a regular in the Second XI. Writing about the Bedsers in his book *The Bedsers – Twinning Triumphs*, Alan Hill commented:

> The burden of the Second XI bowling in 1938 had been shouldered by F.G. Pierpoint, the Bedsers and Stuart Surridge. Phil Mead played for Suffolk against Surrey scoring a century and taking 5 wickets including Surridge.' Through the season Surridge scored 196 runs at 21.77 and took 29 wickets at 23.10. Highlights included a score of 77 against Cornwall at the Oval in a match that was won and an innings and an analysis of six wickets for 89 against Middlesex at the Oval although on this occasion the game was lost. Many of the players previously in the Young Players side had by now graduated to the Second XI, including the Bedsers, Mobey, McIntyre, Whittaker and Constable.

There was still an opportunity to play for the Young Players in five matches scoring 76 runs at 15.20 and taking 10 wickets at 21.70. There was one match for the Club & Ground side and of particular interest he was made captain of one side in the Surrey Trial Match. Either because he was an amateur or because his leadership qualities had been noticed, he captained the team on 28 and 29 April, the other captain being A.T.W. Taylor.

In 1939 he played in only two matches for the Second XI in the Minor Counties Championship during July against Wiltshire at the Oval and the Guildford Club at Guildford, both matches being won although he did not bat in either match and in total took just two wickets for 98 runs. This was, however, after he had made his first-class debut playing for Minor Counties who beat Oxford University at The Parks. In the first Varsity innings he took 5-41 and in the second innings mopped up the tail with a further three wickets for a match analysis of 8-100. He was only required to bat once, scoring 20.

He was heavily involved in club cricket during this period principally playing for Old Emanuel, but also for The Wanderers and Horley. He played for the Club Cricket Conference against UAU at Roehampton, also in July. Players with future connections appearing in this match included A.C.L. Bennett of the BBC and the future Lancashire captain, K. Cranston.

FOUR

The Second World War

Stuart Surridge applied to join the Royal Air Force just before the Second World War in 1939 but was rejected. He then took up farming, which was classified as a reserved occupation throughout the war. He went to work on his uncle's farm at Mucking in Essex, living at nearby South Ockenden Hall. His brother, Percy, ran the farm at Aldermaston.

While living in Essex, Stuart first met his future wife, Betty, at a Farmers dance in late 1941. Betty was not immediately attracted to him but Stuart persisted and they started going out together. Stuart married Betty on 3 April 1943. She was the daughter of Alfred Spicer, who owned a fruit shop in Upminster. His father-in-law was a supporter of Essex cricket but Stuart manfully learned to live with this. Stuart and Betty started their married life at Great Lakes Farm in Horley and after the war moved to Earlsfield Road, where they lived for the rest of their married life.

At the start of the Second World War, Stuart Surridge Ltd had their head office and showroom at 210-212 Borough High Street and factories nearby in Tabard Street and Vine Yard, Marshalsea Road. The company were involved in war production. Having been registered as suppliers to the Admiralty, the War Office and the Royal Air Force they made a wide range of leather goods including flying jackets.

This part of London was in the centre of the area subjected to the worst of the Blitz as it was so close to the docks. It should be recalled how devastating the damage inflicted by the Luftwaffe was: the main

Working on farm with Alan Moss.

attacks lasted from 25 August 1940 to 16 May 1941 during which time 40,000 civilians were killed and 46,000 more were seriously injured. Over one million homes were damaged or destroyed.

There was continuous bombing from 26 August 1940 to 2 November – fifty-seven consecutive nights – there were only three nights in November when the Luftwaffe bombers did not attack London. The 'real' London Blitz finally ended soon after an extremely heavy raid on 10 May 1941 when almost 1,500 people were killed on a single night and the House of Commons was severely damaged. It was one of the most punishing nights London firemen had experienced, and nowhere was it crueller than in Southwark and Lambeth. It started with a heavy fall of incendiaries and high-explosive bombs in the vicinity of the Elephant and Castle, the famous south London pub at the junction of Old Kent Road and Newington Butts. Many buildings were hit and the area had all the makings of a conflagration from the outset. The first pumps to arrive set in to a nearby 5,000-gallon emergency dam while orders were given for water relays to be put in operation from

Wedding.

the Manor Place Baths and the converted basement of the old Surrey Music Hall at St George's Circus, each about 800 yards distant. The first jets emptied the 5,000-gallon dam in just five minutes, bringing fire fighting to a halt until new water supplies became available. Meanwhile, fire crews worked frantically to set in their pumps to the swimming pool at Manor Place and to the basement dam at St George's Circus. Weary firemen somehow found reserves of energy and ran their hose along the kerbside towards the great raging inferno. Then disaster struck. A large high-explosive bomb crashed among the cluster of pumps crowding around the old Music Hall dam, killing seventeen firemen and creating such havoc that access to the water supply was completely blocked. The fire was now out of control and rapidly spreading as the enemy pilots, recognising a prime target, set about stoking it up to even greater fury.

More water relays were put in hand from the Thames at London, Waterloo and Westminster bridges and from the Surrey Canal, over distances ranging from a mile to a mile and a half. Slowly, jets were brought to bear on the fringes of the fire to halt the spread and gradually built up as more hose lines were linked to the Thames. Over 2,000 fires raged over a wide area of the capital and it was on this night that the premises of Stuart Surridge at Tabard Street received a direct hit and was totally destroyed.

Owing to very heavy press censorship by the Government the full extent of the damage inflicted that night was not public knowledge. 11,000 houses had been damaged beyond repair, 12,374 people had been made homeless, 1,800 had been seriously wounded and 1,436 people had been killed. Never in the city's 1,898-year history had so many Londoners perished in one night. And the final death toll didn't include those who died in the days and weeks that followed.

The end of the Blitz saw the start of the reconstruction of London, even though building materials were in desperately short supply. The docks had been devastated, as had many industrial, residential and commercial districts, including the historic heart of the city.

By 1943 the Surridge company had moved into premises at 174 Weston Street, Borough, formerly occupied by William Brock & Co. Ltd, who were leather bag manufacturers. This was a five-storey building mainly used, eventually, for the production of cricket bats. The clefts were delivered to the premises and taken by lift to the top floor. They were then processed down the building to finish as the completed article on the ground floor. During the war, production continued on leather goods for the services.

The Surridge home in Earlsfield was very close to Clapham Junction, a major target for enemy bombers, but no damage was inflicted on the immediate area. Alf White, one of the Surridge company employees, however, was bombed out of his home in Peckham and moved into 28 Earlsfield Road taking a flat on the upper floor.

At the outbreak of the Second World War in 1939, the Oval was requisitioned by the Government and converted into a prisoner-of-war camp in anticipation of invasion by Germany. The playing area was covered with barbed wire supported on concrete posts driven into the ground and huts were erected. The whole place lay idle. There was no cricket, and as there was no invasion by land, sea or air, there were no prisoners. Later in the war, the Oval was used as a site for searchlights to assist in the defence of London from bombing.

The Oval was never the same again. Many a bowler had prayed for it to be dug up. I am sure Bill O'Reilly echoed the sentiment while Hutton compiled his mammoth 364 in 1938, just as 'Bosser' Martin — who in those days prepared his Test match wickets 'to last till Christmas' — gloated as England marched towards a total of 1,000. Martin was probably the only disappointed man that day when Hammond declared at 903. Martin had retired by 1945 and a new groundsman, Bert Lock, faced the formidable task of putting the turf in order again for cricket. Lock soon showed that he had no superior at his specialist position. He scoured the country for the requisite turf for his square, eventually finding it on the Hoo Marshes near Gravesend in Kent. The outfield, formerly as hard as a macadam road, was turned into a lush green pile carpet, and the pitch no longer broke the bowlers' hearts, for he ensured that it gave them all a fair chance. As a result, the Oval shed some of its reputation as a batting stronghold while at the same time increasing the potency of their bowlers.

FIVE

Return to Cricket: 1946–1951

Stuart Surridge did not play for any of the Surrey teams in 1946 but played in nine matches for the Second XI in 1947. Of these matches six were won, two were lost and one lost on first innings. He scored 290 runs at 22.31 and took 58 wickets at 14.67. He played for Old Emanuel during the four seasons up to 1949 although details of his averages are not available. Owing to his Surrey commitments in 1949 the school magazine recorded that: 'His assistance early in the season was most welcome, if not to the opposition.'

His highest scores for Surrey were 72 not out against Gloucestershire, 54 against Yorkshire and 46 versus Norfolk, all at the Oval. His best bowling performances were 7-52 and 5-44 in an impressive win over Wiltshire at the Oval.

Surridge duly made his first-class debut for Surrey against Lancashire at the Oval on 7 June, where he took the wicket of Winston Place in the first innings, in all taking 2-76. When batting he was run out for 28 in a match that fizzled out in a draw. During the season he played six matches for the county first team, five of them in the Championship having gained his place when Alec Bedser was on Test duty. He scored only 116 runs at 16.57 and took 10 wickets at 44.50. Alf Gover wrote at a later date:

I had reason to appreciate his catching at first slip. I had suffered from poor slip fielding throughout my career after Percy Fender retired. When Stuart played a few games with me in 1947 he made an immediate

The 1950 Surrey team, back row, left to right: H. Strudwick (scorer), D.G.W. Fletcher, J.W.J. McMahon, J.C. Laker, E.A. Bedser, G. Whittaker, A.J.W. McIntyre, S. Tait (masseur), A. Sandham (coach). Front row: B. Constable, J.F. Parker, W.S. Surridge, M.R. Barton, L.B. Fishlock, A.V. Bedser, G.A.R. Lock.

impression, taking a 'blind catch' wide on his left-hand side. Thereafter I was always happy to see him standing at first slip to my bowling.

There was also one appearance for the Club & Ground against Purley, a match that was won although Surridge scored only one run out of 198/9 and did not bowl as Purley were dismissed for 86.

With the retirement of Alf Gover, Stuart Surridge took the new ball in 1948 and his performances were good enough to secure him a permanent place in the side. He achieved fine performances at the Oval, where he took 5-50 against Warwickshire and 5-44 against Nottinghamshire, contributing substantially towards a win in each case. In 1949 he fared even better, his 6-49 in the Middlesex first innings and unbeaten 41 doing much towards success over the eventual joint-champions.

Being one of the amateurs in the side, Stuart captained Surrey, in the absence of Michael Barton, in thirteen matches in 1950 and 1951. Surrey won seven of these matches, two were lost and the other four were drawn. Eleven of these matches were in the County Championship, six were won and in the match lost against Glamorgan at the Oval in 1951 Surridge made his highest career score of 87. In the same year he achieved his career-best bowling analysis of 7-49 against Lancashire. Both of these achievements came at the Oval.

By the late 1930s the pitches at the Oval were too good for any set of bowlers to consistently dismiss the opposition twice in three days. Surridge, himself, would be the first to disclaim that he alone was responsible for the transformation of Surrey's fortunes in the 1950s. Peter May wrote in his book *A Game Enjoyed* that:

Between 1951 and 1952 three things happened which combined to have a profound effect on what followed. One was a change in the Oval pitches which in 1951 still retained some of their pre-war perfections for batsmen. The ball began to move about, to turn by the second innings and to have a sort of rounded bounce, not especially quick but useful to good bowlers. The outfield, once rough and brown, was now lush and green, and the ball retained its shine longer. In fine weather not many matches were drawn.

Here, in haste, I must point out that the Surrey bowlers of the day were rightly indignant at suggestions that the pitches were made for them. These implied a subtlety, prescience and a deviousness which Bert Lock and his staff did not possess. We were often told by the groundstaff that they had a beautiful pitch for us that day, a promise which left us somewhat mystified when we found ourselves or our opponents 43/7.

We naturally expected a really good pitch for Alec Bedser's benefit match against Yorkshire in 1953. He had just taken 14 wickets in a Test match against Australia; he was at the peak of his career and a highly respected figure. On the first day 21,000 were present but Jim Laker was turning the ball before lunch. We won, but the match was almost over in two days. The beneficiary, although our second top scorer, was not amused.

The statistics show that our main bowlers took at least half their wickets away from the Oval. The change in ground conditions had been to some extent coming on gradually and was accentuated by the rain of 1952 after the sunshine of 1951.

Douglas Jardine wrote in his 1981 *Wisden* article:

Thus in due course we come to the question of wickets at the Oval nursed and produced by the most successful groundsman in England, Bert Lock. From a batsman's view no wicket has changed more radically since 1939 than that at Kennington Oval. Before 1939 centuries in the second innings were a commonplace; since then they have been very rare indeed. Before 1939 no one could remember when Surrey last had a slow left-hand bowler as a regular member of the team. It is no phenomenon, but merely natural, that wickets over a period not only tend, but do in fact produce just those bowlers best suited to them.

Australian wickets for years have eliminated the medium-pace bowler, just as the Oval up to 1939 eliminated the slow left-hander. Bert Lock, at Kennington, has more nearly than anyone else achieved the four-fold ideal facing groundsmen today. That consists of producing a wicket which, while fair to batsmen, lends itself to definite results in three days while encouraging both speedy and spin bowlers. Neither Bedser nor Loader nor Laker nor Lock objected to bowling on their home pitch.

In the late 1940s and 1950s the County Championship comprised seventeen teams and each county played twenty-eight matches. This meant they played each county at least once and twelve counties were played twice, once home and once away. The points system was very simple, twelve points being awarded for a win, with four points for a first-innings lead in a match either lost or drawn. Points were adjusted for tied matches or a match restricted to one day because of inclement weather. There were no bonus points for batting and bowling as used in the modern game. The matches were played over three days with fixed hours of play with usually three sessions of two hours from 11.30 a.m.

to 1.30 p.m., 2.10 p.m. to 4.10 p.m. and 4.30 p.m. to 6.30 p.m. There was no mention of number of overs to be bowled in the regulations. Crucially, the pitches were not covered, the regulations stating:

> The Pitch shall not be completely covered during a match unless special regulations so provide; covers used to protect the bowlers' run up shall not exceed to a greater distance that three and a half feet in front of the popping crease.
>
> The whole pitch may be covered
>
> (i) no earlier than 11 a.m. on the day immediately preceding a match until the first ball is bowled and
>
> (ii) in the case of a week-end match, provided it is the rule of the ground, when, if necessary, the pitch may be wholly covered from the cessation of play on Saturday until the re-start of play. Such covering, however, is permissible only if the pitch has already been wholly covered as provided in (i) above.

As previously mentioned, Surridge secured his place in the first team in 1948 when he played twenty-three games, twenty of which were in the Championship. He also played for the South of England against the North of England in the Kingston-upon-Thames Festival, where he recorded his best bowling figures of the season with 7-82. In all matches he scored 441 runs at 14.22 and took 64 wickets at 28.59. He was awarded his county cap at Guildford on 23 June. Telegrams of congratulation arrived at the ground, including one from his wife suggesting he should not be too late arriving home.

During the season he played in one game for the Second XI against Gloucestershire Second XI at Bristol in a match reduced to one day because of bad weather. He took 1-105 as Gloucestershire amassed 277/5 and scored 38 out of a total of 164 as Surrey lost by 113 runs.

His 1949 season saw him play in twenty-one first-class matches scoring 300 runs at 11.53 and taking 68 wickets at 26.66 with a best performance of 6-49 against Middlesex at the Oval. A full season in 1950 started with the match for Surrey against MCC at Lord's. Otherwise there was one match against Cambridge University and at the Hastings Festival in September he played two matches, one for South of England against the West Indians and for the Over-32 side against the Under-32. In all, he played thirty-two first-class matches with 438 runs at 10.68, taking 79 wickets at 31.25 with a best performance of 6-55 against Worcestershire, again at the Oval. In between the first-class games he fitted in one game for the Club & Ground against Watneys at Mortlake. In a comfortable win he scored 59 out of 190/5 and took 2-13 as Watneys were dismissed for 157.

During the 1950 season when Michael Barton was not available, Stuart Surridge was called upon to captain the side and first led the team in a Championship match against Essex at the Oval, which was lost by 17 runs. The cousins Peter and Ray Smith helped substantially to win a keenly contested game. When Alec Bedser and John McMahon, Surrey's last pair, came together on the final day, 29 runs were needed for victory. They added 11 before Bedser became over-confident and gave a return catch to Peter Smith. This wicket gave the leg-spinner a match analysis of 13-113.

Against Nottinghamshire at Trent Bridge, Surrey won by nine wickets. Nottinghamshire were dismissed in their first innings for their lowest total in two seasons. Alec Bedser and Laker formed a deadly combination of pace and spin. Steady off-spin bowling by Stocks kept the Surrey batsmen quiet, but all reached double figures before Surridge declared with a lead of 155. Nottinghamshire disappointed in their second innings. Set to get 58 to win, Surrey made light work of their task.

At Old Trafford, the match against Lancashire was drawn. Striking bowling performances featured prominently in an interesting match. In one inspired period, Tony Lock took four wickets without conceding a run, and Lancashire lost five batsmen at 48, though Wharton and Hilton helped to instigate a recovery. Before this drama unfolded, Surrey were also severely shaken. They lost four men without getting a run, and Tattersall celebrated the award of a county cap by taking eight wickets at cheap cost. A century by Parker in the second innings was the best batting in the match. After gaining a first-innings lead Surrey declared, leaving Lancashire 360 to win but the Red Rose county fell 84 short with four wickets remaining.

Back at the Oval, Somerset were defeated by two wickets. The visitors gained a first-innings lead of 81 but when batting again they failed

Ready for cricket with Surrey.

against the slow bowling of Lock and McMahon. On the following morning Redman, bowling at a fine pace, caused Surrey to collapse. Cautious methods availed Somerset little in the second innings, and Surrey, left four and a quarter hours in which to score 224, began by losing three wickets for 51. Contributions from Constable, Whittaker, Clark and Brazier brought victory within sight.

Still at the Oval, Surrey beat Northamptonshire by 13 runs. Set to score 207 in four hours, Northamptonshire were 68/5, then 185/9. Fiddling, the last man, stayed with Nutter till, with only seven minutes of the extra half-hour left the latter fell, caught at mid-off. Surrey, with half the side out, were only 67 runs on at the close of the second day, but Clark, batting stylishly, helped to swing the fortunes of the game.

The match against Cambridge University at the Oval ended in a draw. After an uncertain start Clark hit his first century in first-class cricket for Surrey. Constable and Brazier helped him in stands of 150 and 92. The Cambridge batsmen failed against the fast-medium bowling of Westerman but although leading by 167, Surrey did not enforce the follow-on. Eric Bedser and Fletcher began the county second innings by scoring 170 together, and Surrey declared a second time, but Cambridge could not maintain the necessary scoring rate of 80 an hour.

At Bristol, Gloucestershire were beaten by five wickets. A masterly partnership by Fishlock and Constable enabled Surrey to gain an unexpectedly easy victory after, at one time, seeming to be facing defeat. On a bowlers' pitch, Laker puzzled most of the Gloucestershire batsmen, and he took 6-16 in a spell of eleven overs.

An easy victory over Essex was achieved at Chelmsford by an innings and 37 runs. Failure to counter the clever off-spin bowling of Laker brought about the Essex downfall, but Surrey were also indebted to Fishlock as they achieved a formidable total. On the second day Essex lost nineteen wickets for 395 runs and followed-on 218 behind. Though the extra half-hour was claimed, Surrey could not part the last pair before the close, yet needed only five minutes on the third morning to separate Preston and Cousens.

In 1951 Surridge played in twenty-six matches for Surrey scoring 351 runs at 11.70 and his 54 wickets at 30.70 included one performance of 7-49 against Lancashire at the Oval in early May.

Again the opening match for Surrey was against MCC at Lord's. Other than Championship matches he played for Surrey against the South Africans and Oxford University. He missed some matches in early July following the death of his father on 2 July.

Surridge stood in as captain in only five matches in this season; against Glamorgan at the Oval, Surrey lost by two wickets. At one time on the second day they seemed destined to gain a far easier victory for Surrey, facing arrears of 187, lost six batsmen for 78. Then Whittaker led a recovery and the last four wickets realised 244. It was in this match that Surridge made 87, his highest score in first-class cricket. Ultimately, Glamorgan needed 136 to win. Showers affected the turf and Lock, the left-arm spinner, made the ball turn appreciably but Glamorgan just got home in an exciting finish.

The match against Gloucestershire at the Oval was drawn. A missed catch probably cost Gloucestershire the match, for a weakened Surrey team, going for runs against the clock, lost seven men for 145. Fletcher, who should have been caught on 36, saved the game. Gloucestershire made full use of a batsman's pitch on the first day. The all-round work of Eric Bedser served Surrey well in this match.

Surrey had little difficulty in defeating Oxford University at the Oval by eight wickets. The university side fell below normal standards – except ground fielding. From the start the county held the initiative.

At the Oval, Leicestershire drew with Surrey, who bowled keenly on the first day but later in the match, Tompkin and Palmer put on 236 in Leicestershire's highest stand since the war. Surrey were more enterprising and passed the visitors' total for the loss of only three men. In the final stages, Tompkin drove beautifully and his unbeaten 175 was his best in first-class cricket.

His last match as captain in this season was against Glamorgan at Cardiff Arms Park where Surrey won by five wickets. Effective off-spin bowling by Eric Bedser paved the way for their success. Glamorgan's prospects were bright when Surrey wickets were 137/7 but they reckoned without Laker and Alec Bedser, who added 131 in seventy minutes.

SIX

Appointment as Captain of Surrey

There are two very distinct views to be considered when discussing the appointment of Surridge to the captaincy at Surrey. First, there are the opinions of the Establishment and the committee; secondly the thoughts of the professional players at the club. The Establishment view can be summed up by an article by Bruce Harris in the *London Evening Standard* on 21 June 1949 under the banner heading 'Why always have an amateur captain? Surridge is now to lead Surrey'.

Apparently Surrey must have an amateur cricket captain, whatever happens. That is the only inference one can draw from news issued today that W.S. Surridge, the fast-medium bowler, will lead the county side tomorrow against Oxford University in the temporary absence of M.R. Barton. This is not only Surridge's first appearance as captain; it is his first game in the county Championship this season though he did play for a Surrey XI against the County Association of Cricket Clubs. Last year he played quite a lot – 46 wickets with an average of 27; 29 innings with average 13 and top score 33 not out. I am not questioning Surridge's ability as a cricketer and a captain in suggesting that a professional captain – Laurie Fishlock for example – would have been appropriate on this occasion, I believe such an honour would have been appreciated in the Surrey dressing room.

When Michael Barton, at the end of the 1951 season, felt compelled to give up the captaincy because of the pressure of his business interests, Stuart Surridge was not an automatic choice. The names of two Cambridge University cricketers were mentioned but, happily for Surrey, wiser counsels prevailed. It is understood that W.T. Cook, a left-handed batsman who used to captain the Second XI and a man who devoted many years of service to the Surrey committee, urged his colleagues to place their confidence in Surridge, a home product. He was a unanimous choice.

In the Minutes of the Surrey CCC Cricket Sub-Committee of 11 September 1951, it is stated that:

> A.C. Burnett (Lancing & Cambridge University) has offered to captain the First XI for a period of two to three years. The committee decided to offer the captaincy to Stuart Surridge, but should he not be able to accept due to business or other commitments, they should accept the offer from Burnett. [It must be borne in mind that Stuart's father had died earlier in 1951 and Stuart was now one of two principal directors in the family firm.]

A.C. Burnett had obtained his Blue at Cambridge in 1949 and in later years was known as Anthony Compton-Burnett.

Douglas Miller has written the first book in the 'Lives in Cricket' series for the Association of Cricket Statisticians and Historians. His subject was the Glamorgan player, Allan Watkins, who wrote about Tolly Burnett appearing for the county in 1958 as Glamorgan were looking for a captain to succeed Wilf Wooller on his retirement.

> To muddy the waters there was a comical interlude when a corpulent thirty-four-year-old science master from Eton, Tolly Burnett, was drafted in to play in the last eight matches of the season. Burnett was the not wholly innocent pawn of some of the anti-Wooller plotters, and he was sprung with minimal formality on the Glamorgan dressing room. Here, it seemed, was the heir apparent, someone who might take a year or two on sabbatical to head the county.
>
> To seasoned professional cricketers it was a baffling, even insulting, move. 'I don't know where they found him,' Allan says, 'How they could

ever have thought of him taking over from Wilf! He had no idea of cricket. He batted like a fourteen-year-old. He stood right away from the bat. Where he'd played his cricket I don't know.' It came as a surprise to Allan to be told that A.C. Burnett had won a Cambridge blue in 1949. 'Good God, well he didn't look a cricketer!' With Wooller away for the last two matches, Burnett's talent for leadership were cruelly exposed. The sidelining of Haydn Davies meant that Allan was the skipper's right-hand man. 'I remember he wanted to put himself on to bowl,' he says with incredulity. Seventy-one runs from 11 innings, some ponderous fielding and no obvious tactical insight or understanding of the first-class game's subtleties, spelt the end of any enthronement plans.

Reverting to the decisions being made by the Surrey committee it is difficult to establish what actually happened after such a period of time. Some reports suggest the appointment of Surridge was unanimous, whereas others suggest it was by a single casting vote.

E.M. Wellings writing in the *Evening News* on July 1, 1954 commented:

More than most counties, Surrey remain eager to have a captain from one of the two major universities. They have never yet had a professional captain, though one of their amateurs had to be subsidised. Surridge was at neither university, nor was he at one of the more fashionable public schools and his friends have always felt that he held the Surrey captaincy under sufferance. Surridge was indeed elected captain before the 1952 season by only one vote in committee. His rival was a moderate player, who had no connection with the Surrey club, but he had been to Cambridge and there gained a blue. The player was A.C. Burnett, who was in the 1949 Cambridge side as a batsmen but failed to hold his place the following year, not, it would be thought, a strong enough candidate to press such a good cricketer as Surridge.

Surrey have done some odd things with their captaincy since the war. In 1946, they entrusted it to an unknown, Nigel Bennett. Then they returned to Errol Holmes, who was then on the Surrey payroll as organiser of their reconstruction appeal fund and next imported Barton, whose former county was Norfolk. In the same period there was a move to bring in another player from outside, Hugh Bartlett, who had then

Stuart Surridge at home, awaiting the call to lead Surrey.

recently been dropped from the Sussex captaincy. If Surridge is relieved of his position at the end of the season the game will suffer a big loss.

Of all the county captains, Surridge can least be spared. He has had the little extra which most captains lack and which means so much to a team. He has probably been the best county captain since Robins retired after taking Middlesex to the top of the Championship table in 1947.

When you then consider the views of the Surrey professionals at the time – including the views of Eric Bedser below – the following picture emerges:

Never was the 'family' spirit more in evidence than when Stuart became captain in 1952. The more I look back on that incredible era the more

I appreciate the special relationship which existed between the captain and his players. Indeed it would not be going too far to claim that it must have been unique, for though Stuart was regarded as one of 'us' who had been promoted to the leadership, he still retained that measure of respect that every captain has to have to be a success. Usually a captain is said to be one of the boys and popular, which probably means he can't do his job properly, or is distant and unpopular and failing to get his players behind him. The ideal is hard to find, and there can be no doubt that Stuart's status and attitude were telling factors in Surrey's triumphant years.

When he was appointed there was no uneasy period which follows the arrival of a stranger in the dressing room. We did not have to discover each other, which was doubly important at the time as the captain at the Oval changed in a separate place – a man who could so easily feel apart.

One of the privileges of friendship is a free exchange of views, and our opponents must have been surprised at times there was no hesitation in expressing our opinions. We were never inhibited. We could always tell the captain what we thought of his plans and ideas, and he would be equally honest with us. There was no shortage of plain speaking, and anything said in the heat of battle was forgotten on leaving the field. Consequently there was no rancour. It goes almost without saying that we would never have dreamed of being so candid with some of Stuart's predecessors. But frankness and honesty and an open invitation to speak out was one of Stuart's most inspiring gifts and because he was prepared to listen, he earned our respect.

Sometimes he took our advice; sometimes he didn't. But I think he would agree that he owed some of his success to an attentive ear. He was fearless, obstinate, at times he would not be budged from his viewpoint, and he took the kind of outrageous risks which made the pros wonder if he had been out in the sun too long. Such gambles were undertaken because his faith in the team was unbounded and never wavered. And if the captain felt his team had the ability to justify such faith the players in turn felt they must be good and went out and did their business.

Surridge was invited to take control of the side which had an abundance of talent, yet seemed unable to produce consistent results. When the captaincy was confirmed, it is said that he wrote in his diary 'Surrey will win the Championship for the next five years.' If he did write this, he was right, although the Championship was not only won in the next five years but won for seven years in a row, with five successes under his captaincy. It is for his captaincy that he will always be remembered, even though as a cricketer he was demonstrably more than an average performer, especially as a close-to-the wicket fielder.

Like an earlier Surrey captain, Percy Fender, he controlled every game. Many of his decisions seemed eccentric at the time, but when proved correct only added to his reputation as a forceful and inspirational leader. One match in particular demonstrates his style. In 1954, against Worcestershire at the Oval, the visitors were dismissed for a mere 25 and, just as Surrey were building a commanding lead, he declared at 92/3. Surrey then turned around and bowled Worcester out for 40. He had telephoned for a weather report for the following day and knew that rain was likely. Once again, Eric Bedser recalls:

> Suddenly, to the incredulity of the entire team, Stuart decided to close the innings. If ever there was an eccentric declaration this seemed to be it, the father and mother of an absurd tactical decision…even allowing for the fact that Stuart was never happier than when leading the charge on the field. I doubt if there was a player or spectator on the ground who did not think for once Stuart had overplayed his hand. The rest of county cricket were left to ponder on the facts of the match and possibly to think any captain and team capable of such an audacious act were not going to be deprived of the title.

There were many instances of Stuart ramming home an advantage which bore the stamp of his unconventional thinking. He had, of course, two enormous assets – the players with the ability to support him, and the fact that the majority of the side, who had grown up together, matured at the same time. It is a matter of speculation whether another captain could have taken his advantages with such positive assertion and got the team so solidly behind him. I doubt it.

Beyond argument Stuart, a big man in frame and deed, was one of the breed of great amateur captains and it is a sad and surprising fact

MCC *v.* Cambridge University at Lord's. Surridge is caught at the wicket by M.E.L. Melluish.

that, for all he did for Surrey, he was never given the captaincy of the Gentlemen against the Players in the traditional and much-missed match at Lord's. He would have cherished an honour which he so richly deserved. Maybe today's players would regard such an omission as of little account, but Stuart belonged to the days when the amateur adorned the game and every cricketer worth his salt wanted to play in the traditional fixture.

Stuart was not just an outstanding captain. He was also a fine player, bowling with exceptional hostility with the new ball, hitting lustily as a batsman and excelling in the field. His personal example as a close-in catcher set the standard for which Surrey were famous. Either at short leg or in the slips Stuart took marvellous catches. As befits a crack shot he had a quick eye and there was never a more fearless fielder close to the bat.

He often demonstrated his shooting skill at fair booths and shooting galleries, collecting numerous prizes. Once at Weston-super-Mare he took so many prizes that the proprietor banned him!

Stuart's friendship and loyalty towards his old players has never waned down the years, and there is an ever-open door to them all at Earlsfield Road where he still lives. Alec and I cannot resist the occasional visit to talk over old times and we seldom leave without thinking Betty must have been an unusually understanding wife during the years when Stuart was away so much. At least she seems to enjoy the cricket talk as much as Stuart. Fortunately he did not abandon his love for the game and Surrey when his remarkable playing days finished, for his enthusiasm was then carried to the office of President and as a member of various committees.

To play with Stuart was a vivid experience, the stuff of dreams and it can be said without fear of contradiction that there's only one Stuart Surridge and we shall not see the like of him again in county cricket. A great captain, a bubbling personality who left the mark of his identity on every game in which he played and, definitely, a man's man.

Never a man for safety-first tactics, he went for victory persistently from the first ball. He never jockeyed for first-innings points. If they came, all well and good, but his two main objectives were runs from the batsmen in a reasonable time and all-out attack by the bowlers who were supported by a dynamic set of fielders. Surridge would never tolerate bowling down the leg side to keep down the runs. His main attack consisted of in-swing and off-spin bowling on or just outside the off-stump. From the very beginning Surridge enjoyed the wholehearted support of all his players. As soon as his election was announced, Alec Bedser told him, 'All the boys are one hundred per cent behind you and playing for your side.' No skipper could have had a better endorsement.

He was inspired in the task which lay ahead by a remark passed to him some seasons earlier by Brian Sellers, the great Yorkshire captain. At that time Surrey and Yorkshire were fighting for the Championship along with Glamorgan, Middlesex and Lancashire. Yorkshire had beaten Surrey at the Oval by 73 runs and in the pavilion afterwards Sellers said:

Stuart Surridge leads out his team followed by Peter May, the Bedser Twins and the rest.

'It is no good being second.' This was an approach, Surridge thought, that Surrey needed.

Surridge kept spurring his men along with this phrase. Other pet sayings were 'Someone will get them', when they wanted runs and 'we SHALL bowl them out.' Surridge appreciated the great bowling resources he had at his command and, moreover, realised that these could only be exploited to the full if catches were held. He set out to stress the value of catching by personal example.

The transformation under Surridge was little short of miraculous. Standing 6ft 1½in tall and tipping the scales at thirteen stones, Surridge looked every inch a leader. His infectious enthusiasm inspired the whole side. No one bothered about individual performances and averages; these were merely achieved in the course of events. Surridge believed in the personal touch.

In the 1950s it was the custom for the captain and amateurs to change in different rooms to the professionals and at away matches stay in different hotels. Train travel saw the amateurs in the first-class compartments and the professionals in third-class carriages. Surridge did not agree with this policy, and despite opposition from the committee, ensured that the team always travelled together by train and stayed at the same hotel. If he was hard on his players on the field, all was forgotten at the close of play. For relaxation they indulged in golf, Surridge himself again setting the example with his prodigious driving.

Cricket was never dull under Surridge. In the very wet summers he challenged the clock as well as the opposition. The season of 1954 provided a typical example. When Surrey began their nineteenth match, their Championship prospects looked very thin. With ten matches left they stood eighth in the table, 46 points behind Yorkshire, the leaders. Few people, apart from Surridge and his players, held optimistic views of their chances. Then came a most remarkable change – rising to the heights, Surrey swept all remaining opposition aside. They gathered 112 points out of a possible 120 and finished twenty-two points ahead of Yorkshire, the eventual runners-up.

The retention of the title was achieved primarily through the supremacy of the attack, supported by fielding of uncommon excellence. Allied to this fielding supremacy was the initiative and imagination of

The Queen at the Oval accompanied by the President of Surrey, Lord Tedder, and the captain, Stuart Surridge..

the captain, Surridge, who so accurately assessed the tactical risks and possibilities of each situation.

A true leader, Surridge was always the boss. He would never tolerate any sign of slackness. Even if a player did wear an England cap, he had to perform as Surridge desired. Surridge knew how to cajole his men into action: soft words for some, for others a sharp tongue, but there was never any bitterness.

Tom Clark told a story of when Surridge put him in charge of a tense situation with Derbyshire at Chesterfield in 1952. Surrey were making heavy weather of it against the deadly partnership of Jackson and Gladwin, but at lunch Clark was still there with Laker. Surridge took Clark aside and told him that as the last of the regular batsmen he must take command and get as much of the bowling as possible. Laker was soon out and in came Surridge, saying as he arrived, 'Now you're in charge, Tom, I don't want the bowling.' Surridge, while Clark watched from the other end, proceeded to hit two sixes and six fours, scoring 52 out of 73 in twenty-two minutes. Midway through this display, Tom said, 'Who's in charge here?' only to receive a broad grin from his captain. That stand turned the match and Surrey won by six wickets.

Another example of Surridge's enterprise was provided in the Northamptonshire match at the Oval in 1954. Despite a century by Oldfield, Surrey had dismissed the opposition for 180 and with Peter May scoring 169 they were building up a big lead the next day when Surridge declared at 359/6. 'I am giving them an hour's batting,' he said, 'We can get six wickets down tonight.' As the pitch looked full of runs, this seemed to be the height of optimism, but Surridge was right; at the close of play Northamptonshire were 22/6 and Surridge led his men triumphantly back to the pavilion.

During those five momentous years, Surridge and his men enjoyed many exciting moments. Three occasions remain indelibly stamped on his mind. First, was when they won the Championship for the first time in August 1952. The second was a day in July 1955 when Surrey were playing the South Africans and the Queen, patron of the Surrey club, visited the Oval for the first time.

'This was the biggest thrill of my life, to meet Her Majesty and to introduce the side,' says Surridge. 'She knew so much about the Oval and the people who were playing.' The third was in May 1956 when Surrey became the first county team to beat the Australians for forty-four years, as described in a later chapter.

It must be said that for much of the time he was captain, Surrey were not the most popular side in the County Championship – but then how many winning teams are? At times the aggression shown by the close fielders was greater than many felt to be acceptable. Perhaps this was one reason why he was never chosen to captain any representative sides when he had so much to offer.

SEVEN

Amateurs and Professionals

Roy Burgess wrote an article for *The Cricket Society Journal* of spring 2007 entitled 'Was the Amateur good for Cricket?' which is reproduced here as it sums up precisely the position of amateur cricketers in the era in which Stuart Surridge was involved in the game:

Norman Preston, in his editorial notes to *Wisden* 1963, lamented the abolition of the amateur status in first-class cricket on the grounds that the amateur had played such an important part in its development, that cricket would be in danger of losing the spirit of freedom and gaiety that the amateur had brought to the game and that there could be a detrimental effect in the vital matter of captaincy at county and Test level. It is the purpose of this article to examine some of these issues to discover whether or not Norman Preston's contentions about the amateur's contributions were justified.

One of the main arguments put forward for the amateur status was the claim that the professionals were quite content with their inferior position. Certainly there was no concerted outcry about the situation and it was not until four years after the seismic change introduced in 1963 that the Cricketers' Association came into being and even then not with any notable enthusiasm from the professionals. It was not a great upsurge of democratic fervour that brought about the decision in 1963. Up to the Second World War, the professionals were, by comparison with other employees, reasonably well paid with the expectation of a

tax-free benefit after a certain period of service. Their existence might
have been hazardous; their careers short but in the prevailing economic
climate, the lot of the professionals had its advantages. These factors,
together with an innate British conservatism and deference to the
class system, help to explain a lack of militancy, even fatalism amongst
professionals and their acceptance of the existing power structure.
Moreover, the example of those few professionals who criticised the
system when still employed by their counties discouraged others from
rocking the boat.

When Cecil Parkin in 1924 complained, in a newspaper article,
about the tactics of A.E.R. Gilligan, the England captain, in the first
Test against South Africa, he brought on to his head the wrath of the
establishment and was described by Pelham Warner as potentially, 'the
first cricketing Bolshevist'. The following year Parkin suggested that
either Jack Hobbs or Herbert Sutcliffe should captain England if no
suitable amateur could be found which caused Lord Hawke to have
apoplexy and resulted in his intemperate blast against the very idea
of a professional ever leading the national team. Although Parkin
apologised for his criticism of Gilligan, his career was in ruins and he
soon departed from the first-class game. However, what is significant
about the incident is that Parkin found no overt support for his views
amongst his fellow professionals and he even went on record that he
was in favour of the amateur principle. Jack Williams contends that
cricket reflected the degree of stability within English society in the
1920s and 1930s.

The professionals were no iconoclasts but that does not mean that
they were all as contented with their lot as, for example, Jack Hobbs
and Denis Compton, both of whom stated that they had no problems
with the amateur/professional divide and its consequences (in this
connection, it is perhaps not irrelevant to note that they received
earnings from cricket well in excess of their peers). Polite and discreet
they may have been but, as Tom Dollery pointed out, whilst it would
not be true to say that professionals were embitted by the years of
discrimination which had endured in the most acute form up to 1939,
it would not have been unaffected by it. After Fred Root retired, he
recorded in *A Cricket Pro's Lot* (1937) his resentment of the social

distinctions in the game, whilst Walter Hammond, in 1952, wrote that any professional, if he was prepared to speak out, would admit that the present system was not in the best interests of the game. And George Cox of Sussex voiced his strong opinions about the social divide to a sympathetic David Sheppard. Hammond and Cox, of course, were writing and speaking after the Second World War when, even if at a tortuous pace, the feudal barriers were coming down and deference was not so much in evidence, but their views probably reflected those of the majority who remained silent for the whole of the period up to 1963.

Norman Preston was concerned that the abolition of the amateur 'could have a detrimental effect in the vital matter of captaincy both at county and Test level.' Admittedly there were some outstanding amateur captains: Preston quite understandably refers to Brian Sellers and Stuart Surridge. The obsession, however, with the social status of a candidate for captaincy rather than with his ability to cope with the job cost some counties dear after 1918. Between the wars, Northamptonshire and Worcestershire, in particular, suffered from short-term, stop-gap nonentities (as cricketers) leading the teams, simply because they were amateurs. Unlike Yorkshire, they could not afford such passengers. Even after the Second World War, which had gone some way to the breaking down of class barriers, the practice continued, with such disastrous captains as N.H. Bennett for Surrey and Ken Cranston and N.D. Howard for Lancashire. Rather that appoint a professional captain, other than as a temporary measure, some counties resorted to importing a suitable amateur, as in the case of Charles Palmer who joined Leicestershire as secretary-captain in 1950. As David Lemmon comments, 'Palmer's move to Leicestershire was typical of much that was happening at the time, for whenever a county threatened to have a professional captain it seemed as if some higher authority found an amateur who could be imported and was capable of doing the job.' Jack Hobbs, although quintessentially an establishment figure, stated that many professionals were capable of captaining their counties and should be so appointed rather than inexperienced amateurs who lacked cricketing ability. Yorkshire, as early as 1928, convinced Herbert Sutcliffe possessed leadership qualities, courageously offered him the captaincy of the county. Initially, Sutcliffe accepted. However, after protests about this break in tradition, the Yorkshire committee apparently backtracked and brought pressure on Sutcliffe to withdraw his acceptance. Although he agreed in order to avoid controversy, he never had any doubts about his own capacity as a captain and as Leslie Duckworth states that, in retrospect, Sutcliffe regretted that he had succumbed to the committee's pressure. W.E. Astill, in 1935, demonstrated how effectively a professional could perform as captain. Appointed by Leicestershire, Astill proved an outstanding leader and the county enjoyed, according to *Wisden*, its most successful season ever. This had no influence on the Leicestershire committee as, the next season, the amateur C.S. Dempster of New Zealand replaced Astill. Under Dempster, the county slumped from sixth in the County Championship to fifteenth (winning two games) in 1936 and to sixteenth (winning one game) in 1937. Leicestershire appeared to have learned from this experience, appointing its long-serving professional Les Berry as captain in 1946. His leadership qualities were praised and the county enjoyed its best season since Astill's brief reign. At least Berry lasted three years but was replaced in 1949 by Stuart Symington who led Leicestershire, in his one season, to the bottom of the county table. It was left to Warwickshire to make the decisive break with tradition with the appointment of Tom Dollery as county captain in 1949. This was not a stop-gap expedient and Dollery proved to be an outstanding captain with Warwickshire winning the County Championship in 1951: even *Wisden* admitted that he demonstrated that 'the paid player can become a captain in the real sense of the word'. He raised the status of the professional and at last the *ancient regime* could no longer ignore the fact that some of the peasants were at least capable as their betters in taking charge of county sides. Eric Hollies succeeded Dollery as captain of Warwickshire, whilst Dennis Brookes, Willie Watson, Maurice Tremlett and Don Kenyon all proved to be splendid leaders of their counties. David Sheppard was fully in favour of a professional with the requisite leadership qualities captaining his county commenting, 'When it came to the argument that you needed amateurs to perform the independent captain's role, I can think of some who were complete slaves to their committee and one professional who seemed to be totally independent from his county committee.'

The contempt entertained by many amateurs towards professionals was not confined to the Golden Age. G.O. Allen described Larwood and Voce as 'swollen-headed, gutless, uneducated miners' and he condemned the professionals in the MCC team that toured Australia in 1932/33 as 'a collection of half-wits'. Ian Peebles ridiculed Sutcliffe's bourgeois pretensions, 'He emerged from the First World War an officer, convinced that he could take his place in society and to his end took pains to acquire the accents of Mayfair and Oxford. This attracted a certain amount of ridicule'. Undoubtedly, many amateurs were very class-conscious and regarded the professionals as inferior beings, resenting any attempt they might make to better themselves and obtain middle-class trappings. After the Second World War, A.R. Gover was elected to the Surrey committee but, although he had been commissioned during the conflict, he was treated as untrustworthy by some of the members who suggested, because he was a journalist, he should withdraw from certain meetings. And, of course, he had been a professional.

Up to the outbreak of the Second World War, the amateur/professional divide might be explicable by the social customs of the time, even if not in the best interests of the game. However, the division continued for another twenty years after Hubert Preston, in 1943 *Wisden,* called for 'the total deletion of all distinctions between professionals and amateurs in first-class cricket. To me, at least, such questions as the position of a cricketer's initials and the precise gate from which he is to enter the field have long seemed vastly absurd'. The election of a Labour Government in 1945, committed to wholesale reform and the creation of the Welfare State, had no effect on cricket and Prime Minister Clement Atlee, an enthusiastic follower of the game, was apparently quite content with its exciting power structure. Accordingly, the MCC, as cricket's administrators, was determined that the sport should continue as if the Second World War had not occurred, notwithstanding the beginnings of the breaking down of former class barriers. As late as 1958, the MCC had expressed itself as satisfied with the distinctive status of the amateur cricketer which the Advisory County Cricket Committee (with no professional representation), reporting on the subject, considered was of great value to the game. Thus the full might of the establishment fell upon Jim Laker in 1960 for criticising Peter May in his book *Over to Me*. Shades of Parkin and Gilligan! However, Laker, who had shrewdly published his memoirs towards the end of his active cricket career, was soon forgiven and restored to the pavilions of the Oval and Lord's from which he had been summarily banished after publishing his book. And, as Norman Preston ruefully remarked, by 1962, the opinions of some members of the 1958 Advisory County Cricket Committee had apparently been completely revised. Wisely, these members had recognised the inevitable, i.e. that the amateur status was long past its sell-by date. After all, this was the swinging Sixties and 1963 was, according to Philip Larkin, an *annus mirabilis* with the end of the Chatterley ban and the Beatles' first LP; in so many walks of British life the old order was being replaced, with deference at a discount after the Profumo affair. Hopefully for the better; cricket was simply following the trend.

David Lemmon commented in his book *Changing Seasons* that Surridge played three times for the Gentlemen against the Players, at Scarborough, but it was not a fixture he enjoyed or supported. His heart was with Surrey and he left representative cricket to others. He believed the Gentlemen and Players match to be an anachronism.

Jim Laker commented in his book *A Spell from Laker*:

> Not a single representative honour came Stuart's way, for incredibly there remained at Lord's a hardcore who never regarded him as a cricketer or a captain. There is no doubt that he should have skippered the Gentlemen, particularly when one considers some of the ragbag cricketers selected; and what a good choice he would have made for a minor overseas tour. He certainly did not lose any sleep over it, for he was very much a man of Surrey, where his real love truly lay, and where his achievements were unparalleled.

Stuart Surridge never scaled the heights of Test cricket, nor did he appear for the Gentlemen at Lord's in the annual Gentlemen *v*. Players fixture, although he did appear in three of these fixtures played at Scarborough. This was despite possessing that priceless asset of leadership which turned a capable set of cricketers into a match-winning combination. While Surridge always maintained that 'I am just a club cricketer', of few players would it be more true to say that his bowling and batting figures completely misrepresented his full value to the side.

Douglas Jardine commented in his article for *Wisden* in 1981: 'One may regret that he never had the honour of captaining the Gentlemen against the Players at Lord's; still more that he was never entrusted with the task of taking, and bringing on, an England 'A' team overseas. But Surridge was ever a county man, first and last, and as such can have few if any regrets.'

In 1956 the following letter appeared in the *Daily Telegraph*:

Sir,

The Revd E. Lomax appears to think that W.S. Surridge, the Surrey captain, is deserving of representative honours for his brilliant fielding alone. Your correspondent might pause to wonder why, after six or seven years playing as an amateur, Surridge is the only regular player who has not been 'honoured' with an invitation to represent the Gentlemen. May I suggest three possible reasons? The MCC is not alone in disliking personalities, and Surridge is almost the only personality left in the game. He, not being a university man, does not come within the MCC's definition of a 'gentleman'. And most people are jealous of success.

Yours faithfully,

H. FARMER, London E.C.2.

The obituary of Stuart Surridge in the *Daily Telegraph* on 15 April 1992 included a section written by E.W. Swanton, who was very much a pillar of the Establishment. His comments included:

In the Surrey side he inherited were a few reputedly awkward personalities. They did not remain so for long. In the post-war euphoria big crowds flocked regularly to the Oval to see the attacking cricket on which Surridge insisted. His instinct was aggressive in all respects, especially in the fielding. The strong bowling was supported by four brilliant close catchers Lock, Barrington, Stewart and, not least, the captain himself. John Warr, his opponent in many a tough fight, has described Stuart Surridge as 'an enthusiastic extrovert buccaneering risk-taker'. I would add only that, in truth, the keenness on the field at tense moments sometimes grew rather too fierce – slightly akin to what one deplores today.

EIGHT

Stuart Surridge & Co. Ltd, 1946–93

By the end of the Second World War the directors of Stuart Surridge & Co. Ltd were Frederick Walter Surridge and Percival Surridge, the father of Stuart Surridge. Percival maintained an interest in two farms in Horley, Surrey, and Aldermaston, Berkshire, where willow trees were grown and from which some of the cricket bats were made.

When Percival Surridge died suddenly in 1951 there was a brief obituary in *The Cricketer* which acknowledged his support of the magazine especially during the difficult war period. The management of the company, Stuart Surridge & Co. Ltd, then passed to Stuart and his brother, Percy Clarkson Surridge, who were appointed as directors. Percy travelled abroad establishing contacts and purchasing goods such as hockey sticks from India and Stuart ran the office in London and organised public relations. Every visiting overseas cricket team ended up at a reception at the showroom of Surridge in Borough High Street.

During the years when he was Surrey captain, Stuart Surridge could be found in his office in the Borough from early morning completing a full day's work before leaving for the Oval for the day's cricket. Even then he was known to return back to the office in the evening. By this time cricket bats were being made in a five-storey building at 174 Weston Street in the Borough, having first been occupied in 1943. The local council later placed a compulsory purchase order on this building and production was moved to Witham in Essex during 1968. Only six to eight people moved from the Borough premises despite the generous terms of housing offered for the London overspill town but included the factory manager Fred Simmons, who completed fifty years' service with the company in 1980, by which time production had reached some 20,000 bats a year.

Not surprisingly, many Surrey players used bats supplied by Stuart Surridge Ltd. One of these bats was supplied to Ken Barrington and marketed as the 'Ken Barrington Autograph Bat'. He used to come down to the factory at Witham with Micky Stewart to select his bats. Ken would choose one and then Micky would promptly grab it and then he would have to choose another one. He preferred a light bat of 2lb 3oz without the grip or 2lb 4.5oz with the grip. He never worried about whether it was a wide grain or a narrow grain, as long as the pick-up was right and he liked the balance. Few players looked after their bats as well as Ken. He used to sandpaper the bat down after use and it was as clean at the end of the season as it was at the start. One year when he brought the bat back at the end of the season we found that it was one-eighth of an inch narrower. That doesn't sound a lot but it meant a great deal to these players. Stuart Surridge recalled:

> I cannot remember Ken breaking a bat. He used to chip a bit off occasionally and we would have to repair it. It wasn't unusual for him to use the same bat through a whole season. The bat he was using in the West Indies when he died was a 'Jumbo'. It was not his usual bat but he liked the balance.

Like many great players Peter May would manage to play with any bat but Herbert Sutcliffe and many other players were very obsessive about their bats. Peter May in his book, *A Game Enjoyed* explained 'I have been asked, for example, about the weight of my bat which was 2lb 4oz. Stuart Surridge used to give me two bats at the start of the season. At the end of it, although I would often protest, he took them off to his museum.'

The cutting and splitting of the willow is heavy work and very beneficial in building up muscle for fast bowlers. Many bowlers have used this source reported, for instance, in the *Daily Express* of July 1953:

> Wallington-born Peter Loader was a dental mechanic until Surrey captain Stuart Surridge persuaded him to spend last winter cutting down willow trees. The Surrey captain told the 10st 7lb fast-medium bowler, 'You need to put on weight to be a fast bowler.' Loader did. He is now 11st 4lb., but Surridge says he needs still more weight, wants him to continue the building-up process with willow trees next winter. Frank Tyson was another fast bowler who was to benefit from the 'Surridge winter programme'.

As mentioned in an earlier chapter, cricketers in the past also used this method to improve their fitness.

The company also made cricket balls. The area of the country where cricket balls were made centred on Tonbridge in Kent. New firms joined the old ones, but the men they employed were of course 'the old firm' of traditional craftsmen of the Tonbridge area, which was the reason why the newcomers came there. Stuart Surridge of London came to Tonbridge in 1938 and took one of the houses in the centre of the elegant Salford terrace in Quarry Hill Road which had belonged to a Dr Watts and converted it into a cricket ball factory. It was still there in 1979 beside St Stephen's church on the Tunbridge Wells side of the railway line, as was the whole terrace with its name engraved beneath its central arch but with its fine frontage spoilt by the row of shops at street level. No.19, which became Surridge's cricket-ball works, is now White's.

Stuart Surridge & Co. Ltd managed to carry on throughout the war, and when Fred Sayers was released from his duties as a War Reserve policeman, he joined them as one of the four stitchers on the top floor of the Salford Terrace house, which had a shed in the garden to house the three quilt makers. Bill Ingrams was manager, and altogether there were some twenty-six men making 'Surridge' cricket balls.

After fifteen years of a declining market, the Tonbridge cricket-ball makers decided to apply the Board of Trade's wartime remedy of

Surridge inspecting a bat in the factory. (Photograph from Roger Mann Collection).

concentration. In 1961 the cricket ball departments of Surridge and Ives in Tonbridge and Gray-Nicolls in Hildenborough closed, and they amalgamated with CWS-owned Duke/Wisden as Tonbridge Sports Industries. TSI confined their cricket-ball making activities to the old Duke factory at Chiddingstone Causeway which produced one range of cricket balls but marked 'Duke', 'Wisden', 'Surridge' and 'Gray-Nicolls', each firm marketing its own brand.

The cricket bat manufacturing activities of Stuart Surridge at Witham, Essex, of Thomas Ive at Preston Road, Tonbridge, Gray-Nicolls at Robertsbridge and Duke/Wisden at Chiddingstone

Causeway each continued to operate independently of each other, and of TSI.

On a trip to the West Indies, Stuart saw the opportunity of marketing a cheaper cricket ball. He approached TSI on his return but they were not interested in producing a lower-priced and lower-quality product. Stuart and Percy then set up an agreement in India who were able to supply some 30,000 balls in a very short period of time.

In 1952, the company accountant, Frederick Hopkins, was appointed as a director – the first from outside of the family – who remained on the Board until 1989. In the 1970s the company was flourishing with a substantial export business. The turnover stated in their annual accounts submitted to Companies House rose from £448,176 in 1973 to over £1 million in 1977. It reached its highest level in 1985 at £1,379,295 and then slowly dropped to £984,585 in 1990, the last year that a declaration was made.

Other companies were purchased, including George Clarke & Co. Ltd at Sutton St Nicholas, near Hereford, which specialised in making cricket stumps and balls, tennis racquets, hockey sticks and sledges for winter sports. Another acquisition was R.E. North & Co. Ltd, located in Glossop, Derbyshire, manufacturers of soft leather goods. During the 1970s the company had a majority interest in a Scottish firm, L. Linda Ltd, who made cricket and golf trousers.

Diversifying into other sports the company manufactured footballs. One of their employees, Alf White, was the inventor of the first 'Laceless Football', for which the company took out a patent. This football was made of plastic-coated leather and the importance of this development was phenomenal. The ball was no longer weighty and difficult to control when wet, which meant players with flair could display their full ability. The first use of this football was in the World Cup in Sweden in 1958. England manager Walter Winterbottom took the new, British-made ball with him, which was chosen for the tournament after being tested by catapult and found to travel 20ft further than any of those supplied by the other nations.

In September 1978 the distribution of shares within the company listed Percy Clarkson, Stuart's brother, and Stuart as the main shareholders and their respective sons, Percy and Stuart as minority

Surridge cutting timber.

shareholders. Percy Clarkson Surridge had two sons, Percy Stuart and John. Percy Stuart emigrated to Australia on reaching his twenty-first birthday and took up farming. With the help of the family and a friend, Dr Ron Wambeek, he purchased a farm in Albany, where he stills lives. Dr Wambeek was a medical practioner who had two practices, one in Chelsea and the other at Horley, where he was closely involved with carrying out medical inspections on pilots at Gatwick Airport. Percy Clarkson moved out to Australia to live with his son when he retired in the 1980s.

John, who still lives in Horley but not at Great Lakes Farm, was trained by his father in the art of producing and buying suitable willow trees for cricket bat making and at one time became production manager at Witham. After the business was sold he stayed on at the factory for two or

Talking cricket bats with Mike Proctor and Barry Richards at the Surridge factory during the 1963 South African Schoolboys tour.

three years. He is now self-employed and involved in buying and selling willow for cricket bats for his own company, 'Surridge Willow Services'.

The son of Betty and Stuart was born on 28 October 1951 and named Stuart but is known by his family and friends, as 'Tiger'. In time he became heavily involved in the business. At one stage he was assisting in running the subsidiary company, Richard E. North at Glossop but also had many contacts with county cricketers, supplying them with bats and equipment. By the mid-1980s, Stuart Surridge & Co. Ltd were employing up to sixty-eight staff of whom fifty were involved directly in production.

After Stuart Surridge died in 1992 decisions were taken within the family concerning their futures and Stuart Surridge & Co. Ltd was sold to Dunlop-Slazenger in September 1993, including the use of

John Surridge.

the family name. In 2001 Dunlop-Slazenger sold the Surridge name to an Indian and South African partnership based in Johannesburg who then sold it on to the SDL Group in May 2006. This company is now run and owned by the current managing director Charles Lord and his family, trading as Surridge Sports from their base in Burnley.

The current range of Surridge Sports is listed in three catalogues for cricket, football and rugby, selling the full range of equipment, clothing and accessories. There is no direct manufacturing in the

'Surridge' advert at the Oval.

United Kingdom but they have employees resident in certain countries who are responsible for quality control, etc. The countries concerned are India, Indonesia and China. They are still using some of the manufacturers in India which were set up some thirty to forty years ago. Surridge cricket bats are now made in India but English willow is used for the top quality bats.

Surridge clothing is used by seven out of the eighteen first-class cricket counties with more being approached. Two countries in the 2007 Cricket World Cup, Scotland and Holland, used Surridge clothing. Teamwear is identified as the main business development for the future, with forays being made into professional football. The Championship team Barnsley wore Surridge kits during the 2007/08 season, including in their momentous FA Cup victories over Liverpool and Chelsea.

Stuart [Tiger] then set up a property management company, which he still operates. Betty Surridge still lives in Earlsfield Road.

NINE

The Five Glorious Years

In the five years between 1952 and 1956 Stuart Surridge missed only ten County Championship matches because of injury or business commitments. As is well recorded, this commitment to turning out for Surrey was a significant factor in instilling a team identity and mentality in keeping with their status as perenial champions. The success of the Surrey was not just down to the inspirational leadership qualities of Surridge – a number of other factors can be cited.

The following chapter goes on to outline the consistent nature of those who were to be integral in carrying out the philosophy that embodied the flamboyant, daring mindest of their great leader.

The record of Surrey in this period was:

Year	Won	Drawn	Lost	Played
1952	20	5	3	28
1953	13	11	4	28
1954	15	10	3	28
1955	23	0	5	28
1956	15	7	5	27
Total	86	33	20	139

During these five years, Surrey used twenty-seven players who played in the following number of the matches.

129	W.S. Surridge	82	P.B.H. May	21	L.B. Fishlock
	B. Constable	80	P.J. Loader	19	D.J. Cox
122	T.H. Clark	71	K.F. Barrington	17	J.W.J. McMahon
110	E.A. Bedser	54	M.J. Stewart	14	A.F. Brazier
107	A.V. Bedser	36	R.E.C. Pratt	7	G.N.G. Kirby
	A.J.W. McIntyre		R. Subba Row	6	D.E. Pratt
102	D.G.W. Fletcher	28	G.J. Whittaker	4	M.D. Willett
98	G.A.R. Lock	25	R. Swetman	3	H.R.A. Kelleher
97	J.C. Laker	24	J.F. Parker	1	R.A.E. Tindall

The results of the Championship matches when Surridge was captain are;

Won 79   Drawn 31   Lost 19   Played 129

A further breakdown by years is:

	Home			Away			
Year	Won	Drawn	Lost	Won	Drawn	Lost	Played
1952	11	2	1	9	3	2	28
1953	10	3	1	3	7	3	27
1954	7	2	3	5	7	0	24
1955	11	0	1	9	0	4	25
1956	8	4	0	6	3	4	25
Total	47	11	6	32	20	13	129

Of the 64 home matches, two were played at Guildford, both of which were won, and 62 at the Oval – 35 of these matches were won, 12 by an innings and 17 by more than five wickets. Only six matches were lost, one by an innings. Eight matches finished in two days or less.

The matches played away show Surrey won 32 out of 65 matches with four matches won by an innings and 17 by five wickets or more.

20 matches were drawn and 13 lost, one by an innings. Again eight matches were completed in two days or less.

	Home	Away	Total
Won by an innings	12	4	16
Win by runs	17	10	27
Win by five wickets or more	17	17	34
Win by four wickets or less	1	1	2
Drawn	11	20	31
Lost by an innings	1	1	2
Lost by runs	3	8	11
Lost by five wickets or more	2	4	6
Lost by four wickets or less	0	0	0

The toss was won in 63 matches and lost 66 times. Surrey declared their first innings closed in 32 matches and declared in their second innings on 21 occasions, whereas the opposition only declared their first innings closed 12 times and in the second innings set a target to Surrey on four occasions.

In the 129 matches in which Stuart Surridge played, Surrey cricketers scored 53 centuries and there were 132 instances of five wickets in an innings by the following players:

Total Number of Individual Centuries

13	P.B.H. May
7	T.H. Clark
6	K.F. Barrington, B. Constable, D.G.W. Fletcher
5	M.J. Stewart
3	E.A. Bedser, R. Subba Row
1	L.B. Fishlock, J.C. Laker, A.J.W. McIntyre, J.F. Parker

Instances of Five Wickets in an Innings

44	G.A.R Lock
28	J.C. Laker
26	A.V. Bedser
17	P.J. Loader
9	W.S. Surridge
3	E.A. Bedser, J.W.J. McMahon
1	T.H. Clark, D.F. Cox

Fielding was considered so important in the progress of Surrey and was considered key to their Championship successes. The leading fielders in terms of catches during these five seasons were:

1952　W.S. Surridge, 58 (51); G.A.R. Lock, 54 (50); J.F. Parker 38 (38)

1953　W.S. Surridge, 48 (48); G.A.R. Lock, 36 (31); D.G.W. Fletcher, 27 (27); J.C. Laker, 26 (26)

1954　G.A.R. Lock, 42 (37); W.S. Surridge, 39 (37); J.C. Laker, 29 (29); P.B.H. May 26 (21); M.J. Stewart 26 (26)

1955　W.S. Surridge, 56 (55); M.J. Stewart, 52 (52); G.A.R. Lock, 48 (43); P.B.H. May, 33 (26); J.C. Laker, 26 (24)

1956　W.S. Surridge, 54 (54); G.A.R. Lock, 44 (33); P.B.H. May, 31 (28); M.J. Stewart, 28 (27)

Total first-class catches are main figure with catches for Surrey in brackets.

TEN

1952

One reason for Surrey's tremendous advance was the confident assurance of all the players in their own ability, and for that happy frame of mind they had to thank Stuart Surridge. He believed in playing attacking cricket all the time, and when occasionally things did not go well, he was content to take responsibility. That the Surrey batsmen often hit off runs in the fourth innings on a worn pitch when there would have been every excuse for an inept display was because Surridge insisted that from the start they must try to knock the bowlers off their length.

While capable batting is essential, brilliance in the field usually decides the Championship. This was certainly the case with Surrey. They possessed three England bowlers in Alec Bedser, Laker and Lock, who undeniably made the attack the best in the country. On top of this, the fielding under the inspired example of Surridge can seldom have been surpassed. He set up a new Surrey record by holding 58 catches and, incredibly, another fielder exceeded the half century as Lock held 54 chances.

Anywhere close to the bat suited Surridge and due to his watchfulness, anticipation and agility he pounced on seemingly impossible chances. The Surrey field was traditionally set as follows: Lock excelled at short fine leg with Alec Bedser and Parker in the slips; Laker at gully; Constable and May at cover; and Fishlock and Fletcher in the deep. All played their part in making Surrey a side to be treated with respect by all batsmen.

Such was Surrey's strength they did not concede any points until 13 June when Glamorgan led them on first innings at Llanelli, and not until 18 July were their colours lowered for the first time, by Lancashire. On that occasion, at the Oval, and also when they were beaten away by Warwickshire and Yorkshire, they were without Alec Bedser, Laker, May and Lock, who were engaged on Test duty. In fact, at no time was Surrey's best eleven mastered.

Naturally, the three Test men were the main bowlers. Although absent from nine county matches, Alec Bedser appeared in four more as compared with 1951 and he took thirty-nine more wickets. At times he looked better than ever. Indeed, he had never bowled so consistently well for Surrey, and his form compelled people to compare him favourably with Maurice Tate at his best. Laker, curiously, took twenty-nine wickets fewer than the previous year but at less cost. In any case he showed no decline in effectiveness, and the deficit was offset by Lock, who reached 100 wickets for the first time.

In 1951 *Wisden* suggested that Surrey's batting in 1950 was the weakest in the hundred years history of the club. When Surridge took over the leadership, one of the first problems he had to solve was the choice of opening batsmen. He decided on Fletcher and Eric Bedser and they seldom let him down. In fact, they were generally the leading run-makers. The rehabilitation of Fletcher was one of the features of the summer. Enjoying good health for the first time for some years, he lived up to his early promise and, gaining a regular place, he finished with the highest aggregate for Surrey in Championship matches, scoring 1,325 more runs than the previous season. Moreover, Fletcher was most attractive to watch, for his driving and hooking were always crisp and clean.

After the university match, May was a welcome acquisition, and for the second year he headed the Surrey batting, besides coming second only to his Cambridge captain, Sheppard, in the national averages. For the most part Constable occupied the third place in the batting order and he was equally at home whether defending or indulging in neat, stylish strokes.

Whatever other batsmen accomplished, it was doubtful whether Surrey would have carried off the Championship without the help of

A chance eludes first slip as Surridge looks on.

those two stalwarts, Fishlock and Parker, who retired at the end of the season. Both began the summer knowing that they might, from time to time, have to make room for younger players but their keenness, experience and undiminished skill made them valuable assets when the tension was greatest. Clark, one of the comparative newcomers, also proved extremely reliable and consistent. A man with broad shoulders, he showed promise of becoming a big name in Surrey cricket. Enough was also seen of Brazier to believe he was a batsman with more than average ability. McIntyre, whose victims numbered 70, again kept wicket admirably but his batting fell away, as did that of Whittaker, who did not touch his true form until the Kingston festival in September.

Although Surrey won the title with three matches to spare they had been chased throughout by Yorkshire who finished in second place. When comparing their respective records it will be seen that Yorkshire lost one fewer match but did not convert enough of their draws into wins.

	Played	Won	Lost	Drawn	Points
Surrey	28	20	3	5	256
Yorkshire	28	17	2	8	224

Surrey opened their Championship season with a win in two days against Gloucestershire at the Oval. After steady Surrey batting, Gloucestershire were set 266 to win in their second innings but began disastrously with two remarkable catches being taken by Lock at short leg. They were taken from very hard hits and disposed of Emmett and Graveney. Despite a brisk stand of 60 by Wilson and Lambert, they made no real recovery.

Surrey won their next match at the Oval against Sussex by ten wickets, an outcome of enterprising cricket. Eric Bedser and Fletcher shared a partnership of 162 in the first innings, their highest together, and then knocked off the 71 required in the second innings for victory. A win against Northamptonshire at Rushden was founded on yet another opening stand by Eric Bedser and Fletcher of 94, which turned out to be the only substantial stand of the match.

Back at the Oval, Warwickshire were beaten in two days with the bowlers holding the initiative throughout on turf so loose and dusty that the ball continually turned quickly and hurried through at awkward, varying heights.

The Whitsun match at Trent Bridge was won by 210 runs. Continuing their experiments to find the ideal preparations for the Trent Bridge pitch, the Nottinghamshire committee instructed that the heavy roller should not be used on the selected strip for a week before the game. Consequently, the pitch took spin for the first two days, and on the third Nottinghamshire batted under conditions that made Alec Bedser's fast-medium bowling almost unplayable. The last five Nottinghamshire wickets fell for a mere couple of singles.

After Leicestershire had been set 270 to win at 95 runs an hour at the Oval, rain intervened and permitted only thirty-five minutes' batting in

Surridge about to field the ball at short leg.

their run chase. This had followed centuries scored by Eric Bedser and Constable in the Surrey second innings. The match ended as a draw and, as Leicestershire also drew the return match in September, they alone of all the teams which met Surrey in 1952 avoided defeat in both matches.

Surrey achieved another victory in two days at Bristol against Gloucestershire. In this match, Lock was struck on the head whilst fielding and retired to the pavilion. Later on, Eric Bedser was brought on to bowl and made the ball turn a great deal. This heartening sight spurred Lock into action and, determined not to miss one of life's golden opportunities, was soon seen to be staggering down the pavilion steps to rejoin the game. He promptly took 6-15 in 24 balls, the best bowling performance of his career to that point. In a drawn match at Llanelli, Glamorgan took the first points from Surrey by gaining a first-innings lead of just nine runs on a lifeless wicket producing very dull cricket.

Returning to the Oval, Surrey recorded their first win over Essex since 1938. The match went to the last afternoon with both Laker and Alec Bedser taking five wickets in the final innings. They were both playing for England as Surrey moved on to face Kent at Blackheath and duly registered a win by nine wickets, despite a century by Arthur Fagg. Wright alone caused the Surrey batsmen serious trouble and when he tired, Arthur McIntyre assured Surrey of a commanding lead.

Surrey then won by five wickets against Hampshire at Guildford, but they met stiff resistance and gained their victory with only thirty-five minutes to spare. Their undefeated record also looked in danger, but eventually Surrey were left five hours in which to score 275 to win. They succeeded mainly through the brilliance of Fletcher, who scored one of his finest centuries.

Somerset were beaten at the Oval by an innings and 180 runs in a match memorable for a superb display by Constable, whose 205 not out was the best of his career and the highest of the season for Surrey. On the second day, when only one hour's play was possible, Somerset lost three men for 47 but Surrey were home by 3.30 p.m. on Friday with two hours forty minutes to spare. Making the most of a soft pitch, they captured 17 wickets in three hours ten minutes. Only once in the two Somerset innings did a bowler hit the stumps and altogether 18 catches were held through more brilliant fielding.

Their main rivals for the Championship, Yorkshire, came to the Oval and were beaten by eight wickets with twenty minutes to spare. Surrey were largely indebted to Alec Bedser, who had rarely bowled better. When Yardley won the toss everything pointed to a substantial Yorkshire total but Bedser yorked Hutton with a grand ball and, apart from the left-handers, Wilson and Wardle, the Yorkshire batting went to pieces. Surrey showed more consistency but with Yardley exploiting off-theory, runs did not come easily against Wardle and Leadbeater. At times Eric Bedser drove firmly, but his 89 occupied three hours forty minutes. The best display was that of Brazier, who was taking part in his first county match of the season. Although Surrey led by 148, Yorkshire finished the second day only 16 in arrears for the loss of Lowson, brilliantly caught by Fishlock at square leg, and Wilson, who was dismissed the following ball to a surprisingly fast delivery. Hutton gave one of his best batting exhibitions, but next morning he again fell to Alec Bedser when he turned his back on the ball. Thereafter Yorkshire concentrated on defence, much to the annoyance of a section of the crowd, who indulged in so much barracking when Leadbeater was defying Surrey – he stayed an hour – that umpire Price sat and lay on the grass until the noise subsided. Finally Surrey wanted 102 in one hundred minutes and, with Fishlock and Eric Bedser hitting freely, the task was accomplished with twenty minutes to spare.

Their winning ways continued against Worcestershire at Kidderminster with a relatively easy win by ten wickets. On a pitch sparsely covered with grass, their spin bowlers, particularly Lock, held the key to victory. Parker and Clark laid the foundations of Surrey's success in a stand of 127 for the fifth wicket. Worcestershire, 126 behind on first innings, were beaten as soon as Surridge turned to his vaunted spin attack. Half the side went for 98 and the last five wickets fell for 41; Surrey hit off the 14 runs required with twenty-five minutes of the second day to spare.

The most enthralling match of the year was when Kent came to the Oval. So marked was the tension in the final minutes that the crowd rose to their feet and a burst of cheering broke out as Surridge made the winning hit with the clock pointing to a shade after half-past six. The events of the last innings showed that against a side prepared to accept the challenge, Murray Wood's declaration – which set Surrey 188 to win in ninety-two minutes – gave Kent an even chance. Although wickets fell frequently, Surrey pursued their aggression to the end without regard to the risk of defeat. They required 128 in the last hour, 50 with seventeen minutes to go, and 26 when the eighth wicket went eight minutes from time. Surridge, the next man in, scored from eight of the nine balls bowled to him, but before he slashed Dovey over extra cover for the final stroke he and Clark were both missed in the deep. With less than a minute left and the game still open, Kent raced into position and Dovey hurriedly bowled the first ball to ensure another over.

In total contrast, the visit of Lancashire to the Oval was a disaster as Surrey lost by an innings and 70 runs. With May, Alec Bedser, Laker and Lock engaged on Test match duty, Surrey lacked the confidence to face up to Lancashire and suffered their first and heaviest defeat of the summer. On a green pitch always helpful to the faster bowlers, Surrey were made to fight hard for runs on the first day when Statham maintained a particularly accurate and hostile attack. On the second day Washbrook and Edrich wore down the Surrey attack and Place, Grieves and Howard pushed home the advantage with strong driving. Against the pace and lift of Lomax, who gained his best bowling figures for his county, and Statham, Surrey offered only feeble resistance on the last day.

Although Test call-ups again deprived Surrey of their England players, Middlesex were beaten at Lord's by nine wickets as they played aggressive cricket throughout. Loader, who made the ball run away, did well as opening bowler. Eric Bedser in the first innings, and Clark in the second, bowled off-breaks admirably. Fishlock, missed when on 14, played forcing cricket in one of the best innings of the summer for Surrey. He and Parker provided an entertaining partnership and the veteran left-hander finished with 95. Apart from Brown, Middlesex batted with little confidence on a sporting pitch, although Bill Edrich, employing a runner, was typically courageous in his resistance. Fletcher and Constable made light of Surrey's task to achieve victory, scoring 116 together in seventy-five minutes.

Despite the absence of nearly half their regular team, four of whom were engaged in the Gentlemen *v.* Players match at Lord's, Surrey gained a comfortable victory over Sussex at Hastings after some splendid cricket by both teams. Stylish batting by Constable and Brazier, who added 95 at a vital period on the first day, held Surrey together before Surridge, driving with tremendous power, hit a six and nine fours in an exuberant display. Sussex batted inconsistently against the speed of Loader. In their second innings, Surrey sacrificed wickets in the interest of quick scoring and left Sussex to make 321 in five and a quarter hours. When six men were out for 140, Sussex seemed doomed, but two youngsters, Parks and Suttle, made a bold bid for victory by adding 91 in fifty-five minutes. At tea, when two hours remained, the Sussex total was 231/6 but immediately after the break, Loader upset Suttle's off-stump. Lock, who had been released from the Lord's match after extensive protests by Surridge, then had Parks lbw and on his departure Surrey soon finished off the game.

The Queen's Park ground at Chesterfield was packed on the first two days by enthusiastic crowds, who saw Derbyshire give the Championship leaders a hard fight. In keeping Surrey in the field until past 5 p.m. on the opening day, Derbyshire had to thank Elliott, Willatt and Morgan, who batted splendidly against keen bowling and fielding. Missed catches proved expensive to Derbyshire when Eric Bedser and Parker were given early lives, for while Bedser resisted stubbornly, Parker played a great attacking innings, being particularly severe on Gladwin. Their stand yielded 126, and Surridge later hit with such power that – with two sixes and six fours – he reached 50 out of 73 added with Clark in twenty-two minutes. Subsequently, Derbyshire followed Surrey's bold methods with determination and Hamer and Revill put on 84, but a collapse followed; by the end of the second day the home county were 59 ahead with only four wickets left. Strong driving by Rhodes prolonged the issue on Friday, but, thanks to a sparkling stand of 107 by Eric Bedser and Fishlock, Surrey won comfortably. Despite a severe blow on the nose when keeping wicket on the Wednesday, McIntyre, after visiting hospital, continued to play.

The traditional Bank Holiday match against Nottinghamshire at the Oval was won by an innings and 80 runs. Alec Bedser found the pitch affected by frequent showers greatly to his liking. His second-innings figures of 8-18 runs were the best of his career, and enabled him to complete 1,000 career wickets. Remarkably, they had all been taken since 1946. Nottinghamshire contributed to their own downfall by adopting a timid approach to their batting to which Surrey provided a strong contrast, particularly Clark, who stood up courageously against the hostile Butler when the conditions were difficult after a long delay caused by rain. On the second day, between more interruptions from the weather, May and Parker also batted with determination and skill. Nottinghamshire again collapsed badly, their last six wickets falling in an hour on the final day for just 23 runs.

Against Middlesex at the Oval, Surrey won by eight wickets with seven minutes to spare. Owing to rain, the match did not begin until 12.15 p.m. on the second day and although the ball seldom

Stuart Surridge presents his winning team from the players' balcony at the Oval.

lifted, bowlers generally held the upper hand. After Edrich won the toss, half the Middlesex side fell to Alec Bedser and Surridge before Laker and Lock completed the collapse. In both innings Surrey were greatly indebted to the veteran Fishlock. When three hours remained for play and half the Middlesex team had gone for 86, Surrey looked to be winning comfortably but they were nearly thwarted by Denis Compton, who defended splendidly for two hours fifty-five minutes. Consequently, Surrey wanted 101 in seventy minutes. The final rolling left the pitch comparatively docile and fearless hitting carried Surrey home. In a thrilling partnership, Fishlock and May hit off the last 60 required in just thirty-three minutes.

Surrey, requiring eight points to make certain of the title, dismissed the reigning champions Warwickshire at Coventry for a modest total, but threw away this advantage by a sorry batting performance. The Surrey attack lacking Alec Bedser, Laker and Lock – away with May on Test duties – strove to regain the initiative. However, largely through Gardner, who carried his bat, Warwickshire built up a commanding position. Dollery was able to declare and Surrey, faced with the task of getting 350, never seemed likely to succeed once the opening stand had been broken by the means of a foolish run out.

Still without their Test players, Surrey were outplayed almost throughout by Yorkshire at Headingley, but made a gallant late recovery which gave the home side something of a fright. Surrey looked hopelessly placed at the end of the second day when, after collapsing to Burgin and Wardle, they needed 98 to avoid an innings defeat with three wickets left. Next day, however, 173 were added, Brazier and Surridge responding with a stand of 101. Yorkshire needed extra time before winning.

So it was back to the Oval where, on 22 August, Surrey beat Derbyshire by 212 runs to become champions for the first time since 1914 and the first time in normal circumstances since 1899. In 1914, the Championship was awarded to Surrey although their programme had not been completed because of the outbreak of the First World War. Not until 3 p.m. did the turf recover sufficiently to permit cricket on the opening day, and after a stand of 42 for the first wicket, bowlers took command for a long time. Fletcher batted nearly two and a half hours but only he and Parker could do much with the bowling of Gladwin. Then the bowling of Lock, who also made another three remarkable catches, brought about a Derbyshire collapse. Constable, in stands with Fletcher and May, did much to enable Surrey to declare first thing on the third morning, leaving Derbyshire to get 308. From a bad start Derbyshire made no kind of recovery against an inspired Alec Bedser backed by the usual smart fielding, and the match ended five minutes before lunch.

It was then down to Southampton for a comfortable victory against Hampshire, an occasion lit up by another Peter May century. Hampshire never looked like setting Surrey a difficult fourth-innings task. The spin of Laker and Lock carried too much guile for most of the batsmen and, with Fletcher setting the pace, Surrey gained a comfortable victory. At the Oval there followed a drawn match against Northamptonshire where Surrey made good use of winning the toss.

Fletcher, Constable and May contributed the runs so Surridge could declare, leaving Northamptonshire 282 to score at the rate of 84 an hour. Brookes took up the fight splendidly for eighty-five minutes but after he was dismissed Northamptonshire were content to play for a draw.

A classic 197 by May overshadowed everything else in the final Championship match of the season at Leicester. Again Surrey bowled and fielded with unfailing keenness, but the Leicestershire third-wicket pair, Tompkin and Palmer, shaped finely in their sixth century partnership of the summer and saved the match without difficulty.

Surridge enjoyed himself in the festival game at Kingston-upon-Thames, playing for the South against the North. His was an all-round performance: with his batting Surridge hit three successive sixes off Ikin and on the second day took seven catches fielding at slip and short leg.

Looking at the Surrey averages for the season, May headed the batting with 952 runs at 68 followed by Fletcher with 1,886 at 39.29, Constable 1,677 at 36.45, Clark 1,410 at 36.15, Eric Bedser 1,694 at 35.29, Parker 1,204 at 32.54 and Fishlock 1,032 at 29.48. Three bowlers took over 100 wickets in the county season: Alec Bedser, 117; Jim Laker, 102; and Tony Lock 126. Significantly, the next highest wickets tally was Stuart Surridge with 76.

ELEVEN

1953

In carrying off the Championship for the second year in succession, Surrey achieved the distinction their superiority over all other counties merited. After a good start to the season, they lost the lead in the Championship on 11 June and found the challenge of Sussex, Lancashire, Leicestershire and Middlesex so keen that they did not regain it until 25 August. Three days later they emerged supreme on the eve of the final engagement against Hampshire at Bournemouth.

Compared with the previous season, Surrey could only accumulate 184 points and the number of victories dropped from twenty to thirteen. Various reasons accounted for the decline: early in the season it was plain that the batting was suffering from the loss of experience and enterprise of Laurie Fishlock and Jack Parker, who had both retired. Although Peter May, having graduated from Cambridge, was available from the beginning of the summer, he did not find his best form immediately, and not until Subba Row joined the side after the university match did the middle-order batting become at all stable.

There were early indications that Surrey would again make a bold bid for the title for, after being beaten by MCC and the Australians, they overwhelmed Warwickshire in a single day in the middle of May, but further evidence that all was not well with the batting came in the Whitsuntide match at Trent Bridge, where, set to score 198 in three hours, they made no attempt to attack some intelligent bowling and left the match pointless.

Yet a week later at Old Trafford, Surrey gave possibly their best performance of the whole summer in recovering so well from a perilous position that they beat Lancashire by eight wickets. This was typical of their inconsistent form. The weather interfered with some matches, but the biggest handicap was the call on players for representative matches. Often the side were deprived of Alec Bedser, Laker, May and Lock. In addition, Lock, in continuously ripping the ball to spin it, split the first finger of his left hand and missed so much of the summer that he appeared in only eleven Championship matches. Owing to his quality, however, these appearances still brought him 67 wickets.

Possibly the main difference between Surrey and their chief rivals were the number of capable players they had in reserve. The club reaped the reward of their foresight in maintaining an adequate groundstaff at the Oval under the able coaching of Andy Sandham. Also Surrey had the honour of giving four men to England when the Ashes were wrested from Australia in the final Test at the Oval.

Surridge must be given special credit: in his two seasons as captain he had twice steered Surrey to the top. Occasionally he felt compelled to adopt a cautious attitude in batting, the away matches against Middlesex and Sussex provided the main examples, but generally he expected his men to enter all phases of the games in a hostile mood and – like all good leaders – he always set the right example himself.

The bowling was undoubtedly the main strength once again and it was brilliantly supported by the close fielders Surridge, Lock, May and Laker, as well as McIntyre, the wicketkeeper, and Constable at cover. While the three England men – Alec Bedser, Lock and Laker – formed the main part of the attack, five others in Loader, McMahon, Surridge, Clark and Eric Bedser helped to maintain the high standard. The advance of Loader in his second year as a professional was one of the features of the season. For a fast bowler he appeared to be rather frail but he enjoyed a remarkable spell of success between 8–17 July when in three matches he took 34 wickets for 271 runs at an average of 7.97.

When Laker was in form, he twice did the hat-trick, so there were few opportunities for Clark and Eric Bedser, yet when the need was urgent, both bowled their off-spinners with excellent purpose. Similarly, McMahon, having reverted to orthodox slow left-arm, proved a valuable understudy to Lock. This was not enough exposure to first-team cricket and, as he could not expect to hold down a regular place in the Surrey team, decided to join Somerset, where his ability would bring him greater reward.

May again headed his county's batting. When one recalls his struggle in the early weeks to find any sort of form it seems surprising that his final full aggregate of 2,554 runs was 56 more than in 1952. This was a critical summer for May. He lost his place in the England team after the first Test at Trent Bridge, but he played so many fine innings for Surrey that he was recalled for the final Test and fully justified the choice. None of the professional batsmen enjoyed quite the same success as in 1952. Constable was consistently reliable when many of them were out of form in the early part of the season and Fletcher rarely failed. He batted particularly well against the Australians; Clark, after breaking a finger, became established as his opening partner. Eric Bedser shed so much of his enterprise that he dropped to lower in the order. From the time he joined the side at Birmingham on 8 July, the Surrey-born Subba Row solved the problem caused by the loss of the left-hander Fishlock. Himself a natural left-hander, Subba Row made 808 of his season's total of 1,823 runs in county matches for Surrey. Both he and Loader thoroughly deserved their county caps which were awarded just before this memorable season for Surrey ended.

Members rose as one when the triumphant Surrey team walked from the field having begun their Championship programme with victory in a single day. The last and only time that a first-class match had been completed in one day at the Oval was in 1857. Special applause was accorded to Alec Bedser who, in all, took 12-35, and Laker, who performed the hat-trick. Bedser bowled magnificently when play commenced at noon. Unable to obtain a proper foothold on the wet turf, he attacked the leg stump at below normal pace and, helped by fine catches, he equalled his previous best analysis of 8-18. Surrey also found the pitch treacherous but, chiefly through a sound innings by Constable, they took the lead with only two wickets down. The score

Surridge is bowled.

then went from 50/2 to 81/7 and only the aggressiveness of Surridge, who hit three sixes in four balls from Hollies, rescued the situation. Laker and Lock enabled them to gain a substantial lead. Lock became the second highest scorer before a blow above the right eye meant a visit to hospital and his retirement from the game. Laker was called into the attack for the first time when Warwickshire batted again and he began the final rout by achieving the first hat-trick of the season. Warwickshire, batting for ten minutes of the extra half-hour, were all out in seventy minutes, five minutes less than their first innings. No Warwickshire batsman was bowled during a day in which 29 wickets fell for 243 runs – a fact that emphasised Surrey's excellent fielding.

The next match, also at the Oval, was against Gloucestershire. An interesting finish seemed likely until bad light and persistent rain ended play with Surrey needing 192 to win in two hours. Gloucestershire had been dismissed for 220 and Surrey responded with 245, including a breezy 53 from Surridge. In their second innings Surrey were set to get 257 in three hours, and after a steady start, accelerated the scoring until the weather broke.

Another draw was recorded at Trent Bridge against Nottinghamshire. A storm made the pitch difficult on the last day and, after Surrey lost their last five wickets for 20 runs, Laker and McMahon routed Nottinghamshire. Surrey were left to make 198 in three hours but with Dooland again in good form the task was too much for batsmen who lacked initiative.

Surrey then won at Taunton where Surridge declared, setting Somerset 297 to win in five-and-a-quarter hours. Surridge proved the trump card for Surrey, after dismissing Gimblett he took two wickets with the new ball and made a slip catch to end the match with forty-five minutes to spare. Surrey ostensibly triumphed through superior teamwork.

During the previous winter Surridge had been predicting that Surrey would win the Championship in 1953 by 12 points. When the team came back to the dressing room after beating Lancashire at Old Trafford by eight wickets he exclaimed, 'Now we shall win it by twenty... I wasn't expecting twelve points here.' They ultimately won the Championship by sixteen points!

This was possibly the champions' best performance of the season. In any case it went a long way towards them winning the title again for Lancashire, who pressed them so close for so many weeks, could have done with the twelve points which looked to be within their grasp in the early stages of this match. Lock made a welcome return to the Surrey team and not only did he bowl splendidly in the first innings; he also fielded superbly at short leg, holding seven catches. By staying three hours for the top score, Geoff Edrich contributed most towards Lancashire scoring 255. When half the Surrey team fell for 49, the position was retrieved by May, who gave another of his best displays. McIntyre hit fearlessly, and finally Alec Bedser and Surridge gave Surrey the ascendency by putting down seven Lancashire wickets for 43. Although Hilton hit nobly, Lancashire could leave their opponents only a comparatively easy target for victory.

Surrey triumphed against Derbyshire at the Oval on a bowlers' pitch after using ten minutes of the extra half-hour on the second day. Alec Bedser, very lively on drying turf; Lock, with quick leg-spin, and Fletcher, who drove beautifully in the last innings, were Surrey's match winners.

Another draw at the Oval against Northamptonshire. Surrey held the upper hand for two days, but after compelling Northamptonshire to follow on 181 runs behind they dropped Livingston (7) and Barrick (0) in the slips and each stayed for three hours and forty minutes. The splendid bowling of Lock on a perfect pitch was the feature of the second day, but few people at the time realised what this effort would mean to England and Surrey for the remainder of the season. Lock, in spinning the ball for long periods, split the first finger of his left hand and withdrew from the Test team.

The loss of the second day through rain made a draw inevitable at Brentwood, where Essex provided the opposition. Essex batted unevenly and no one dealt surely with the bowling of Loader and McMahon. Surrey failed by eight runs to gain a first-innings lead despite Loader scoring 44, including three sixes and three fours, in just twenty-seven minutes.

Surrey were back to winning ways against Kent, and completed the match with half an hour to spare. The batting of the two sides provided a tremendous contrast. At various times the pitch was subjected to rain but it never became treacherous. Eric Bedser took four slip catches on the last day. Still at the Oval another hat-trick – this time by Alec Bedser – in the second innings could not bring Surrey victory and Essex, helped by rain which eventually stopped the game, foiled their rivals in extra time. Play in the closing stages went on so long in rain that spectators watched from under their umbrellas. Rain also interfered with play on the other days.

Defeating the Champions in well under two days, Derbyshire achieved their best performance of the season at Derby. From the start Surrey were in trouble, for on a pitch suitable for seam bowlers Gladwin and Jackson dismissed eight men for 33 runs. Then Surridge counter-attacked furiously and scored all except four of 55 runs added while he was at the crease. Derbyshire batted much more consistently against the powerful and varied Surrey attack but Surrey once more collapsed in their second innings.

The next match was at Guildford where Sussex won by seven wickets. Excellent all-round work, which included a series of fine catches, contributed to their victory. Sheppard, a model of technical correctness, dominated the occasion and batted more than four-and-a-half hours for his 105. This was easily the best performance of the season by Sussex, who eventually finished runners-up to Surrey. The question was now being asked whether Surrey were on the slide.

The next match was the visit of Yorkshire to the Oval for the game Alec Bedser had allocated for his benefit. Superior all-round form brought them this easy victory, but most prominent was the excellent off-spin bowling of Laker, who took 10-105. Although handicapped by a sore finger, Lock also bowled splendidly. The Yorkshire spin bowlers never exploited the conditions in the manner of the Surrey pair, but there was some admirable fast bowling by Trueman after Surrey had dismissed Yorkshire for 137 – the same total as in 1952. A sound stand of 86 between May and Clark enabled Surrey to take the lead with six wickets in hand and Alec Bedser celebrated by making his top score of the season (45) as he and Laker added 79. Only a masterly display by Hutton saved Yorkshire from defeat in two days. Surridge claimed the extra half-hour without success, but on the third morning the last four wickets fell for the addition of just 34 runs. On Saturday the crowd of 21,000 gave £492 to the collection boxes for Alec Bedser. Altogether, the benefit raised £12,866, easily a Surrey record.

But Surrey failed to win their next two games at Edgbaston and Blackheath. Fast bowlers dominated in the first game in which Warwickshire gained some compensation for their defeat at the Oval earlier in the summer. Surrey appeared destined for a long period in the field when Gardner and Horner opened with a century partnership. A fine spell of right-arm fast-medium bowling by Loader, however, transformed the trend of the innings. Aided by a blustery wind, the young Surrey bowler attacked the stumps with such persistence that seven of his eight victims were clean bowled. Pritchard also gained plenty of life off the pitch and Surrey were always struggling. The manner in which Warwickshire collapsed in their second innings was clearly a portent of what was to follow for Surrey, who crumbled before the hostile combination of Pritchard and Grove. Surridge was not playing against Kent who, having been dismissed for 63 in the first innings, recovered to amass 323 in the second.

The Surrey team of 1953, left to right, back row: A. Sandham (coach), P.J. Loader,
R. Subba Row, E.A. Bedser, G.A.R. Lock, T.H. Clark, J.C. Laker, H. Strudwick (scorer),
S. Tait (masseur). Front Row: B. Constable, A.J.W. McIntyre, P.B.H. May, W.S. Surridge,
A.V. Bedser, D.G.W. Fletcher..

He was back to lead the side to victories against Worcestershire and
Leicestershire at the Oval. The fast bowling of Loader, who surpassed
recent successes by taking 8-21 in the Worcestershire first innings, and
the spin bowling of Clark and McMahon were the deciding factors.
Loader so disconcerted Worcestershire on the lively turf that he clean
bowled five. When they followed-on after more rain the damp pitch
proved more suitable for the slow men and McMahon turned the ball
so abruptly that in one deadly spell after lunch on the last day he sent
back three opponents for a mere two runs.

Surrey were well on top throughout the game with Leicestershire.
In just over three hours before a storm ended play on the first day
Leicestershire made only 71/6, and altogether they batted four-and-

a-half hours for 107, Lester occupied all but ten minutes of that time for 51. Surrey batted much more brightly, with May and Subba Row each displaying sound defence and attractive strokes. Brisk batting by Fletcher and May in the second innings brought victory with plenty of time to spare.

Down at Bristol, Surrey lost again, this time to Gloucestershire. The match was notable for a remarkable performance by David Allen, at the time an unknown seventeen-year-old off-spin bowler. Less than four hours' play was possible on the first day because of rain. Young and Crapp put on 98 for Gloucestershire's second wicket, but Loader worried most of the others. Surrey struggled on a difficult pitch, particularly after May was dismissed. Gloucestershire, 56 ahead, scored quickly and declared leaving Surrey to get 209 to win. This was far beyond them, for Allen made the most of a drying pitch and was almost unplayable.

In the Bank Holiday match at the Oval there was one of the most exciting finishes of the season. On the Saturday, when the pitch was sodden and much time was lost, Surrey concentrated on defence, but the sun shone on the last two days when both teams played grand cricket. May played two fine innings for Surrey, scoring 208 without being dismissed, and Simpson and Clay gave Nottinghamshire a fine start to their first innings. Surrey owed much to the tenacious bowling of Lock. Surrey set Nottinghamshire 209 to make in two-and-a-quarter hours, the rate being 93 runs an hour. At once the visitors accepted the challenge. Clay, driving and cutting brilliantly, hit 58 in sixty-eight minutes. His stand with Poole produced 62 in half an hour. Despite the loss of wickets, Nottinghamshire never gave up the quest for runs. The final over came with the last pair of batsmen together and seven more runs wanted to win. The first ball settled the issue. Giles, acting as runner for Kelly, called Rowe for a single, but Subba Row flung the ball to McIntyre before Rowe got home.

Playing against Hampshire, apart from the first morning when they lost half their side for 61, Surrey never looked in danger of defeat. After Shackleton caused the early batting breakdown with a fine spell of new-ball bowling, Subba Row, aided by McIntyre and Laker, brought about a fine recovery. Harrison and Eagar scored all but 41 of Hampshire's reply which left Surrey 112 ahead. Hampshire were eventually set to get 254, and though Hill and Horton played well they could only delay Surrey's victory.

Having played two more games than their rivals, Middlesex led Surrey in the Championship when their match at Lord's took place. For two days the cricket was worthy of the two leading teams in the country. May played magnificently for Surrey. At the wicket for four hours, this innings helped considerably towards him regaining his place in the England team for the final Test. Denis Compton also batted splendidly, ensuring that late on the second day the Middlesex total reached 227/5. Middlesex were all out for the addition of 19 runs. In fourteen balls, Laker, who turned his off-breaks a foot or more, took four wickets for 10 runs. An enterprising stand of 134 by Clark and May put Surrey completely on top, but after lunch on the third day both sides preferred to play for safety. Their tactics earned much disapproval from the crowd. Except for two overs by Moss first thing, Titmus and Young bowled unchanged from 11.30 a.m. till 3.47 p.m. when Surridge declared. No attempt was made to attack the batsmen and the field was set entirely to save runs. Finally Middlesex faced the almost impossible task of making 287 at two runs a minute. During the three days, over 65,000 people were present, including 15,000 on the last day when the cricket certainly did not provide the entertainment the large crowd deserved.

Cricket enthusiasm was never higher than when Surrey travelled north to Loughborough. With both sides striving for Championship honours, Leicestershire struggled hard against the eventual champions, and managed to restrict them to taking four points from the match. On the second day, aided by lapses in the field, Subba Row and Eric Bedser added 196 for the fifth Surrey wicket and put their side into a strong position. When Alec Bedser took the first three Leicestershire second-innings wickets with only 37 scored, Surrey seemed to be heading for a comfortable victory, but Palmer, Jackson and Smithson, by stern defence, succeeded in saving the match.

Rain reduced the match at Headingley to one of no decision. Too much time was lost for even first innings points to be accumulated. A storm washed out play after lunch on Monday, and on Tuesday Surrey batted carefully until Subba Row and Whittaker added 80 in an hour.

Yorkshire claimed the extra half hour but three wickets remained at the close.

Yet another draw followed at Northampton. Twice Surrey declared in an attempt to force a victory but rain interfered with the game and after claiming the extra half hour they were compelled to rest content with first-innings points. Fine batting by Subba Row, who scored 179 in the match for once out, helped to put them in a comfortable position. When Surrey declared a second time Northamptonshire were left 256 to win in 170 minutes, and although four wickets were down for 132, at 6 p.m. they saved the game without further loss.

The big bowling guns were back for the match against Middlesex at the Oval. After a bad start on a pitch affected by an overnight storm they gained a firm grip on the game. May, who batted almost without fault, completed 2,000 runs for the third successive season. Set 256 to win, Middlesex failed against the spin bowlers and totalled a mere 120.

Glamorgan then came to the Oval and, already weakened by the absence of Wooller and Watkins, they were further handicapped when Parkhouse hurt a foot and could not bat in the second innings. They never seriously extended Surrey, who were without May. After a cautious start on the first day, Clark hit powerfully and his 186 was the highest score of his career. Glamorgan were always struggling but a last stand of 27 enabled them to save the follow-on. Surrey again began slowly, but on the last morning Fletcher was in great form. Set to get 318 in 290 minutes, Glamorgan broke down following a third-wicket stand of 68; the next six wickets fell for 46 and the Welshmen lost the match by 172 runs. This was Surrey's last home match and they were still not champions.

The next round of matches saw Surrey at Hove, where failing to win meant that Sussex lost all hopes of the Championship and left Surrey sure of retaining the title in a drawn match. They celebrated their win by outplaying Hampshire at Bournemouth, who were beaten with a day to spare. Hampshire experienced the worst of the conditions, for, having lost the toss, they batted first on a rain-affected pitch which was ideally suited to Lock. He had all the batsmen guessing and took 8-26, the best figures of his career. Surrey also found runs difficult to obtain particularly off Burden, an off-break bowler from Southampton making his second county appearance. Burden did most to limit Surrey's lead to 69 but Hampshire lost half their side while clearing these arrears. Lock again proved the most successful bowler and he finished with the excellent match analysis 13-69 off 51 overs with 29 maidens. He also took a remarkable one-handed diving catch off his own bowling when he dismissed Rayment for the second time in the match.

Again May headed the batting averages with 2,048 runs at 58.51 and was supported by Subba Row with 827 at 51.68; Fletcher with 1,696; Constable 1,538 and Eric Bedser 1,039. Laker was the only bowler with more than 100 wickets with 115, but Alec Bedser took 98, Lock, 84 and Loader, 80.

TWELVE

1954

When Surrey began their nineteenth Championship match at the end of July their prospects of becoming the first county for fifteen years to win the title three times in succession looked extremely slender. With ten matches to play they stood eighth in the table, 46 points behind leaders Yorkshire. Even though Yorkshire had played two games more and few except the Surrey players thought much of their hopes. Moreover, nor were they playing in the manner of potential champions.

In his book *A History of County Cricket – Surrey*, Gordon Ross recalled:

One day in 1954, Stuart Surridge was driving me home from the Oval. I said to him, 'Stew, you honestly don't believe that you have any chance of winning the Championship this season, do you?' For a moment, I thought he was going to stop the car and ask me to get out. 'What are you talking about?' he replied. 'Of course we shall win it.' And they did! I have never asked any more silly questions!

By playing consistently dynamic cricket, Surrey swept aside all remaining opposition, taking 112 points from a possible 120 and finishing 22 points ahead of Yorkshire, the eventual runners-up. In that period of thorough domination, Surrey raced to five victories in two days and the only game they did not win outright was that against Middlesex at the Oval, in which rain virtually turned the match into a one-day fixture. In a way they might be deemed fortunate that during the closing weeks of the season the weather held them up less than most counties and, in general, the toss favoured them, but those were minor reasons for their success. Above all, the retention of the title came about through the supremacy of the attack, supported by fielding of uncommon excellence, together with the initiative and imagination of the captain, Surridge, who so accurately assessed the tactical risks and possibilities of each situation.

What is even more worthy of record is the fact that this was achieved during a period of extremely bad weather, and Surrey beat the elements on more than one occasion, purely because they finished some matches in two days. Frequently, on what would have been the third day, the rain came down.

Of few players would it be more true to say that his batting and bowling averages completely misrepresented the full value of Surridge to the side. Surridge thought and acted in terms of attack from the first ball and once again the force of his drive inspired his men. A typical example of his initiative occurred in the match with Middlesex early in August. Surrey needed every point possible to keep alive what appeared to be a faint chance of winning the Championship and, when rain limited play to three-quarters of an hour on the first two days and prevented a start before lunch on the last, their hopes of taking any points from the match looked remote. Surridge was not prepared to regard the position as hopeless. Surrey responded to his call for aggressive batting and, following a declaration, they bowled out Middlesex for 51 in two hours ten minutes, with quarter of an hour of extra time remaining. In the field Surridge, holder of 38 catches that season, remained as big an inspiration as ever.

Nothing throughout the summer was more ironic than the fact that almost immediately being passed over for the MCC tour of Australia, the Surrey slow bowlers – Laker and Lock – jumped from ordinary to masterful form. In the last ten games, in fact, the pair took 103 wickets between them, Laker getting 54 and Lock 49, both for an average of less than nine runs apiece. Team after team tumbled before their expert exploitation of pitches offering encouragement and incentive to bowlers with command of length and variation of spin. Loader – who played in the last Test and reached an aggregate of 100 wickets in a season for the first time – and Alec Bedser helped form the strongest bowling quartet in the country against which any batsman could be proud of a long innings. Among many notable achievements by the Surrey attack was the dismissal of Worcestershire at the Oval for 25 and 40 in a match in which the aggregate of 157 was the lowest recorded for any completed County Championship engagement in history.

For several seasons one of Surrey's problems had been to afford adequate opportunity to the many young and talented players on the staff. Successive defeats in mid-season from Yorkshire and Glamorgan led to the recall of Barrington, who had previously just played an occasional game, and the provision of first-class experience to Micky Stewart. Both seized their chance handsomely. On his return to the side, Barrington, a strong, forceful batsman, scored two centuries in his first three innings and Stewart, a neat player with an extensive range of strokes, made two three-figure scores in his first four innings in big cricket. These two gifted batsmen, eager to hit the ball hard, held their places until the end of the season, and their fielding, particularly that of Stewart, made them worthy regular members of such a strong and well-balanced eleven.

Of the established run-getters, none gave more pleasure to spectators or more discouragement to bowlers than May, whose batting in May and June, when he scored over 1,000 runs in sixteen innings, showed how appreciably he had matured during the previous winter's MCC tour of the West Indies. May ran into a comparatively lean spell during Surrey's match-winning climax. However, with most of his colleagues then playing so splendidly, his temporary loss of touch caused little concern and he was never anything but an automatic choice for Australia; he was duly appointed vice-captain to Hutton.

The power of Surrey's reserve strength was adequately reflected by the Second XI winning the Minor Counties Championship, and the double triumph, in which youth played so vital a part, suggested a happy future for the county.

The Championship season had started with a notable defeat as Warwickshire became the first side to beat Surrey at the Oval since July 1952. To provide his out-of-practice team immediate sight and feel of the ball before facing a powerful attack, H.E. Dollery sent Surrey in to bat on an easy-paced pitch and alert fielding and accurate

Surridge catches another one at short leg.

bowling kept them defending. After early setbacks a stand between the
two Dollerys helped Warwickshire to a lead of 27, and Spooner shone
with the ball in the Surrey second innings. A sore shin prevented
May from taking part in his side's second innings, when Subba Row
carried off the batting honours.

Surridge did not play in the next match at Leicester, where Surrey
established a dominating position but rain robbed them of victory.
Normality returned at Hove, but only just, with Surrey winning by one
wicket right at the death. Sussex, well served by Cox and Langridge,
held the whip hand for long periods but Surrey deservedly won.
Through declarations Surrey were set to make 240 in just over two-and
-a-half hours. Surrey fell behind the clock before enterprising batting
by Constable, Barrington and Laker carried them to success.

Having dismissed Northamptonshire for 180 at the Oval, Surrey
were piling on the runs when Surridge suddenly exclaimed: 'I'm going
to declare now and give 'em an hour's batting – we can get six wickets

down tonight.' At the close Northamptonshire were 22/6. The easy win was completed the next morning.

Rain badly affected the next two games against Somerset at Taunton and Glamorgan at Pontypridd which were both drawn. A closely fought drawn match involving Kent at the Oval went down to the wire. On the last day cultured batting by Fagg led the way in an attempt to score 260 to win, but after numerous changes of fortune they required 44 in twenty minutes from the last pair – Witherden and Wright – who averted a possible hat-trick by Loader. They fell short by just thirteen runs.

Still at the Oval, Somerset started well in reducing Surrey to 85/5 before there came a strong recovery by McIntyre, Subba Row and Loader. For the first time in the season, Alec Bedser showed his best bowling form and Surrey led by 146. Then came capital batting by May, who hit hard and cleanly. On the last day Loader and Alec Bedser set too many problems for most of the Somerset batsmen, as Surrey cruised to an easy win.

Rain prevented play on the last two days of the Whitsun match against Nottinghamshire at Trent Bridge, but the first was memorable for superb batting by May. Such was his mastery on a good pitch that he hit two sixes and thirty-two fours in five hours at the crease scoring 211 not out. His innings was characterised by magnificent driving. Clark, who helped to add 140, also batted well. It was on to Old Trafford for the Lancashire match where rain again seriously restricted cricket. The first innings were not completed and the match was drawn.

Back at the Oval, Yorkshire won the match with seven minutes to spare. They gained an early grip which they never lost. Sutcliffe and Wilson scored cleverly and Lester drove with such freedom that he hit seventeen fours in a stay of two-and-three-quarter hours. Apart from Fletcher, most of the Surrey batsmen fared indifferently. Though 151 ahead, Yorkshire did not enforce the follow-on. They too found runs hard to get, but declared leaving Surrey a target of 273. Illingworth, with his off-breaks, caused much trouble and though rain threatened to interfere, he came out with the best analysis of his career taking 8-69.

Another defeat followed at the hands of Glamorgan who won by 110 runs. In a low-scoring match, Surrey were eventually set 187 to win but were dismissed for 76 with McConnon taking 7-23. No points were then gained in a drawn match against Yorkshire at Bramall Lane which again succumbed to the weather.

Then followed an excellent win over Gloucestershire on the team's return to the Oval. Maiden Championship centuries by Barrington and Laker and stylish batting by Stewart pulled them round after the fast bowling of McHugh brought him the first six wickets to fall for just 33 runs. The stand of 198 by Barrington and Laker fell six short of a Surrey eighth-wicket record. Emmett and Milton similarly retrieved Gloucestershire's fortunes, but after another impressive innings by Barrington, Gloucestershire could not withstand the spin of Laker backed by fielding and catching which surpassed even Surrey's normal high standards. Stewart ran out the opening pair with lightning throws from square leg and he held two dazzling catches.

Two draws followed against Essex at Colchester and Kent at Blackheath. Stewart, scoring his second century in successive innings, saved Surrey on the first day at Colchester. Doug Insole, scoring an unbeaten 172, saved Essex similarly when Loader looked like carrying everything before him. Clark dominated Surrey's second innings. Needing 252 to win, Essex began badly but in the absence of Loader with a wrenched ankle, Williams made the game safe.

The loss of the second day through rain prevented Surrey gaining full reward for superior cricket in the Kent match. They batted splendidly on the first day when Stewart began the punishment of Kent's bowlers, which culminated in a last-wicket stand of 71 in forty-five minutes. Rain constantly interrupted the last stage and after being given a good start by Fagg, Phebey and Allan, making his county debut, Kent collapsed against the spin of Lock.

A heavy thunderstorm on an already damp pitch ended play after lunch on the first day as Surrey outplayed Essex in their next match at the Oval. Next afternoon, Alec Bedser, Laker and Lock took full advantage of turf affording them help and Essex lost their last seven wickets for 41. Smith bowled off-breaks effectively, but aggressive batting by Stewart, Clark and Barrington resulted in Surrey obtaining a lead of 109, and the spin of Laker and Lock again proved too much for Essex. Laker took 10-92 in the match.

Nottinghamshire were then easily beaten by ten wickets. Despite a recently fractured finger, Simpson played the Surrey fast bowlers more convincingly than anyone. In the first innings, in which he was last out, he held out on a helpful pitch for two hours and twenty minutes. Apart from Constable and Barrington, few of the Surrey batsmen were able to master the leg-spin of Dooland and Goonesena. Loader, who altogether took 9-64, caused a second Nottinghamshire collapse and the match ended by mid-afternoon on Monday. Afterwards, the teams played a 20-overs game to entertain the 12,000 crowd. Here was a sign of the future. Not the first 20-overs match to be played but it was an excellent attitude towards the paying public.

Middlesex were the next visitors to the Oval. At this stage Surrey needed every point to keep alive their apparently slender chances of taking the Championship. When rain limited cricket to three-quarters of an hour on the first two days and caused a hold-up after lunch on the third, their hopes sank. The increasing awkwardness of the pitch, on which Clark alone played the off-breaks of Titmus with assurance, prompted Surridge to declare. Supported by first-rate catching, Lock and the Bedser brothers put out Middlesex in two hours and ten minutes, with a quarter of an hour of extra time in hand; enough to gain first-innings points.

Six Championship matches remained to be played and Surrey won the lot. Despite being without May and Loader, who were playing in the Oval Test, Surrey proved much too strong for Leicestershire at Leicester. On the first day Laker and Lock made good use of a drying pitch and the home team were dismissed in three hours. Surrey quickly overtook the Leicester total, Constable displaying a wide range of strokes in his century. Rain prevented play until 4.30 p.m. on the second day and Surrey, having declared 79 ahead, attacked hard. Alec Bedser's control of swing and pace and Lock's spin soon dismissed Leicestershire for a second time, and Surrey, although they lost four wickets, won comfortably.

It was on to Cheltenham for the match against Gloucestershire. Ten runs behind on the first innings, Surrey hit back in the style of Champions and finished the match ten minutes before a heavy downpour saturated the ground. The well-controlled medium-fast bowling of McHugh again upset Surrey on the first day but Gloucestershire, against a varied attack smartly supported in the field, fared little better. Barrington, driving hard, and Subba Row put Surrey on the road to success with a fifth-wicket stand of 142 and when Gloucestershire were left to make 269 in four-and-a-half hours on a none too easy pitch; Surridge and Alec Bedser settled the issue. Surrey won by 156 runs.

The spell away from their so-called favourite home pitches continued with success at Worcester by ten wickets. The match provided a triumph for Loader, who took 14-111. He made the ball come sharply off drying turf at the start and only Broadbent, unbeaten after nearly four hours, prevented a complete collapse. Good batting by Clark and McIntyre allied to brisk work for three-quarters of an hour by Alec Bedser enabled Surrey to lead by 95. Then Loader dismissed the first four Worcestershire batsmen at a cost of three runs, and there came no recovery.

An even more comprehensive victory by an innings and 19 runs followed against Middlesex at Lord's. Brilliantly supported in the field the spin bowlers, Laker and Lock, proved too good for hesitant batsmen on a drying pitch. The Surrey policy of sending in their opposition was well rewarded. They dismissed Middlesex before lunch and found conditions easier afterwards. May drove with power and Surridge and McIntyre hit lustily. Facing arrears of 136, Middlesex were again easy prey for Laker and Lock, who although handicapped by drizzle, flighted and spun the ball cleverly.

One of the most famous of Surrey matches then took place at the Oval. Worcestershire were the visitors and Surrey won by half-past twelve on the second day, thus making sure of their third successive Championship. They won in little over five hours of cricket as play had begun at 2 p.m. on Wednesday. In a hundred minutes Worcestershire, sent in on a rain-affected pitch, were dismissed for 25, the lowest score in first-class cricket since 1947. Against Laker and Lock, their last seven wickets fell for five runs. To everyone's surprise, Surridge declared with an hour remaining and a lead of 67. His bowlers left Worcester 13/2 overnight and the next day they spent only an hour in finishing the game as Worcestershire managed only 40. Lock's figures – 6-8 in the match from 15.3 overs – were remarkable.

Surrey welcomed Lancashire for the last match of the season and won by 93 runs. Although the firm pitch played truly in unusually fine weather, bowlers held the key. Statham, much too fast and accurate for most of the Surrey batsmen, twice hit May's middle stump. In the first Lancashire innings Laker received moderate opposition except from Wharton and Washbrook. Strong driving by Clark and a ninth-wicket stand of 56 by Alec Bedser and Lock atoned for a Surrey first-innings collapse. On the last day Lancashire wilted against the spin combination of Lock and Laker.

Again May headed the batting averages with 1,212 runs at 57.71 but Clark, with 1,456, and Constable, with 1,363, passed the 1,000-run mark. The four principal bowlers for the season were Laker with 132 wickets; Lock, with 118; Alec Bedser, with 99 and Loader, 92.

THIRTEEN

1955

Surrey, desperately pursued by Yorkshire, won the Championship for the fourth consecutive season and Stuart Surridge, as their captain, achieved a feat that had only twice been accomplished. Yorkshire, under A.B. Sellers through 1937–46, and Nottinghamshire, under Alfred Shaw between 1883–86, had been successful captains for four years in a row. Moreover, Surrey set new points records for 28 matches, with their total number reaching 284 and they also set the record for number of Championship victories with 23.

Yorkshire, too, surpassed their previous best in both points and victories, but they simply could not overtake Surrey, whose objective throughout the season was to strive for decisive results. In the days when so many sides made first-innings points and immunity from defeat their first consideration, it was most refreshing to find Surrey going through the summer without once being engaged in a drawn match. They played 34 matches, won 27 and lost seven. If winning the toss was a secret to success, Surrey would have failed miserably, as between them Surridge and May lost it twenty-three times.

Surrey began well by winning their first twelve engagements. These included victories against Cambridge University and one against MCC. Their first defeat came in the middle of June in the return match against Yorkshire at Headingley. The second setback provided the sensation of the season when on 12 July, the lowly Kent team overcame Surrey at the Oval. But Surrey remained at the top of the table throughout – indeed,

Stuart Surridge presents Arthur McIntyre to the Queen at the Oval watched by Peter May, Alec Bedser, Eric Bedser and Jim Laker..

only for four days during the four months of the season did Surrey yield the first position to Yorkshire (at times they were bracketed together) and that was at the end of July following defeat by Warwickshire at Coventry.

Later, in the absence of May, Laker and Lock – on duty in the final Test – Surrey failed against Northamptonshire at Northampton and, after they had clinched the Championship against Sussex at the Oval on 26 August, they suffered the anti-climax of losing two of their last three matches to Hampshire at Bournemouth and The Rest at the Oval. Their other defeat was at the hands of the South Africans when, to the delight of everyone associated with Surrey, their patron, the Queen, attended a match at the Oval for the first time.

Surrey again mainly owed their success to their brilliant work in the field, where Surridge once more set a wonderful example by his enthusiastic and enterprising leadership and his splendid catching. As many as seven Surrey players appeared for England (Yorkshire provided six), but thanks to their capable understudies, Surrey were usually able to fill the gaps adequately, although for the most part the batting was thin in the absence of May.

The bowling averages clearly revealed Surrey's strength. Between them the four England players, Alec Bedser, Lock, Laker and Loader took 422 wickets in the Championship compared with 375 in 1954. Although Alec Bedser no longer claimed a regular place in the Test side – he only played at Old Trafford in 1956 – his value to Surrey remained undiminished for he was consistently good. Lock enjoyed his best season, altogether taking 216 wickets.

After his success in Australia, May returned to his best form but his appearances for Surrey were restricted as he had the honour of leading England in all five Tests against South Africa. He headed both the first-class and Surrey batting averages. The two fresher batsmen, Barrington and Stewart, scored many more runs than hitherto and firmly established themselves in the county side. A solidly built cricketer with a deadly aim in the field, Barrington hit the ball really hard. He began the summer so well that he was chosen for the first two Tests but although he made top score in England's disappointing first innings at Lord's, he did not retain his place. Still, Barrington was always a potential run-getter and at the end of the season the Cricket Writers awarded him their trophy for the most promising young player of the year.

Stewart had to wait for his opportunity but he soon became a regular member of the team. He hit his two centuries – 118 against Kent at Blackheath and 104 against Leicestershire at the Oval – in successive matches in the first week of July. Like Barrington, Stewart showed himself to be a forceful and enterprising batsman and both stood out in this most excellent of fielding sides. In fact, in all matches, Stewart, with 52 catches; Surridge, with 56; and Lock, with 48; shared the honours for snapping up close-to-the-wicket chances.

Barrington catches one at silly mid-off watched by Surridge from first slip.

McIntyre not only enjoyed a highly successful benefit year financially but celebrated it with many fine performances with the bat, as well as behind the stumps. His aggressiveness in the middle of the order often helped to turn the tide of a match and he gained the distinction of being the season's leading wicketkeeper with 85 victims. When Evans was injured, McIntyre proved a worthy deputy at Headingley as England's wicketkeeper but, in turn, McIntyre was hurt and consequently the selectors would not risk him for the final Test.

Constable alone took part in all the Championship matches, scoring 1,029 runs which compared favourably with his work of the previous summer. At first, Surrey depended on Clark and Fletcher as their opening batsmen but neither flourished on the lively Oval pitches. Partly because of hip trouble, Clark played in six fewer matches and his aggregate fell by nearly 800 runs, a factor which was offset by the advance of Barrington and Stewart, but there were important occasions when Clark took wickets with his off-breaks. Eric Bedser did useful work as an all-rounder when he returned to the side midway through the season.

After comfortable wins against Cambridge University at Fenner's and MCC at Lord's, Surrey opened their Championship season against Gloucestershire at the Oval with a win by eight wickets. In a match dominated by bowlers, Lock and Loader served Surrey admirably. Rain the day before the game began and a well-grassed pitch provided ideal conditions for them, especially against batsmen who, apart from Mortimore, showed little initiative. For Surrey, Barrington, Surridge and Loader revealed welcome enterprise. On the last day, Surrey, after taking the last five wickets for the addition of 21, began the task of scoring 32 with a heavy thunderstorm approaching. In the quest for runs they lost their opening pair in the first over and they still wanted three when the rain came but Constable promptly hooked Cook to the boundary to settle the issue.

Somerset were then beaten by an innings and four runs and were completely outplayed. The match was a triumph for Lock, who took 11-78. The pitch was damp enough to help the bowlers and Lock achieved bounce as well as spin.

Moving across the river to Ilford, Surrey won against Essex just before another heavy storm broke. Lock played a big part in the success, taking nine wickets and some superb catches. Chasing 150 to win, three Surrey wickets fell for 25 but May and Barrington added 62 before McIntyre, observing the darkening rain clouds, decided the issue with some powerful driving.

In an amazing match at Leicester, despite remarkable all-round cricket from Palmer, Surrey, although behind on first innings, won comfortably. On drying turf Leicestershire began well on the first day but the left-arm spin of Lock brought about a collapse. Then Palmer, bowling medium pace with great accuracy and bringing the ball back sharply off the seam, so severely troubled the Surrey batsmen that he took eight wickets before conceding a run; he hit the stumps seven times. Remarkably, Palmer only put himself on to bowl to change ends for one of his main bowlers. Alec Bedser and Lock troubled Leicestershire in their second innings but Tompkin and Palmer resisted strongly. Palmer, defending skilfully, stayed for four hours but all his efforts were for nothing, as in the fourth innings May, Clark and Constable carried Surrey to victory by seven wickets.

Surrey gave a vastly superior display against a disappointing Lancashire side to win by an innings and 143 runs on their home turf. On a pitch which helped him to move the ball sharply, Alec Bedser caused a collapse at the start, taking four wickets for seven runs in one spell. Apart from Statham, Lancashire also bowled below form and Surrey quickly established a firm hold on the match. Barrington overshadowed May's 122 in an unbroken fourth-wicket stand of 218 and his 135 was then the best of his career. Lancashire again failed in their second innings.

Against Nottinghamshire at Trent Bridge, Surrey finished the match with a hurricane display when set to get 188 in two hours. The Surrey attack met with its first check of the season on the opening day when Simpson stayed for four hours and thirty-five minutes for a round 100. Surrey began shakily before a crowd of 25,000 on Whit Monday, but Barrington and McIntyre added 177. McIntyre took only 108 minutes to get his century and Barrington obtained his second hundred in successive innings. He was awarded his county cap during the innings. After consistent Nottinghamshire batting and a declaration, Surrey went for runs and McIntyre again showed grand form. He and May added 149 in fifty-seven minutes and Surrey won with thirty-three minutes to spare.

After two days of tediously slow cricket, bold hitting by Fletcher and McIntyre carried Surrey to their seventh successive victory with fifty minutes to spare when Glamorgan came to the Oval. Excellent fielding and defensive bowling tied Surrey down on the first day so that even May found few opportunities to display his strokes. After a bright start by Parkhouse, Glamorgan failed completely against controlled swing bowling by Surridge and Alec Bedser on the second morning and were all out in under two hours. They gave a more resolute exhibition after following-on 183 behind and until McConnon and Davies came together they concentrated on defence. Surrey, left two hours twenty minutes in which to score 105, also had to contend with the rain, which fell heavily while Fletcher and McIntyre hit off the last 55 runs in twenty minutes.

The meeting of Yorkshire and Surrey, these two great rivals for the Championship, inspired crowds of Test match proportions to attend on the first two days and altogether 45,000 people paid to see the action. A collection for McIntyre in his benefit match on the Saturday yielded £535. With the ground saturated, Yardley sent in Surrey and they were all out in two-and-a-half hours, the batsmen being helpless against Appleyard, whose rising off-spinners made his leg-trap a persistent danger. With Hutton bowled for a duck in his second consecutive innings, Yorkshire, for whom Watson batted admirably, took three hours to gain the lead. Every ball mattered and no one complained that six hours' cricket on the first day yielded only 193 runs. Lock bowled magnificently for Surrey and in dismissing Lowson made a marvellous right-handed return catch while lying across the pitch. Batting a second time, Surrey exercised great care, Fletcher taking four-and-a-half hours over 84. May alone showed attacking enterprise. More rain changed the conditions on the last day and when play was resumed after an hour's delay, Yorkshire were trapped on a difficult pitch. Alec Bedser always troubled them but Sutcliffe showed great defensive skill for two hours twenty minutes until Bedser pulled off a grand left-handed return catch. The match provided something unique in the appearance of two current England captains, May and Hutton, serving under their two official county captains, Surridge and Yardley.

Surrey were also put in to bat by Essex at the Oval but the result was the same as Surrey won by 62 runs. On the first day, Surrey found run-getting difficult on turf affected by midweek rain and, despite an opening stand of 55, lost half their wickets for 130. Thanks to hard hitting by Laker and Lock and steady play by Constable, the last five wickets realised 113. Though Insole batted skilfully, Essex were 100 behind on the first innings and Surrey in turn fared badly against the fast-medium bowling of Preston. Left 210 to get, Essex began disastrously, but Barker batted skilfully and Taylor stayed with Insole while 57 runs were added before unluckily playing on. Then came another collapse and, though Smith punished Laker for 18 in an over, the last five wickets fell for 35.

It was with a great deal of confidence, then, that Surrey travelled to Headingley for the return match with Yorkshire. This thrilling struggle between the two leading sides in the country drew over 60,000 people and the atmosphere again resembled that of a Test match. Surrey struggled hard to preserve their record but were beaten for the first time in sixteen consecutive games, their previous defeat being in July 1954. The gates were closed on Saturday when 35,000 saw Surrey fight back after losing their first eight wickets for 119. Lock and Loader, who added 96, each made his highest career score. Loader and Alec Bedser completed the recovery with a last-wicket stand of 53. Yorkshire found runs hard to get against accurate bowling, but Wilson defended well for nearly three hours and helped to save the follow-on. Surrey, leading by 102, then broke down completely in the last 100 minutes on Monday, losing seven men for 27 runs in poor light against the fast bowling of Trueman and Cowan. Next day the last three wickets added 48 and Yorkshire needed 178 to win in three hours ten minutes. Until the last half-hour they were behind the clock but they eventually obtained the runs with eleven minutes to spare.

Surridge was absent from the Surrey side when they met Northamptonshire at Guildford where Alec Bedser took over as captain. He was able to celebrate a win, as a result of a declaration, with seven minutes of extra time to spare. This was despite the fact that the first innings had not been decided until noon on the last day. Responding to the Surrey first innings of 346/7 declared, Raman Subba Row, in his first appearance against his old county, scored 112 as Northants totalled 313. In their second innings they were set to make 225 in two-and-a-half hours and they clearly set out to achieve this target. After a determined vigil by Des Barrick his effort was not enough as Laker and Lock twisted out the tail.

Surridge also missed the next two matches against Worcestershire at the Oval and Kent at Blackheath. Both resulted in easy victories with Surrey losing only five wickets in each match.

For the second time during the season Leicestershire worried the champions. Lester, who batted for five hours and forty minutes, made his highest score and he and Smithson – by adding 123 – took part in the first three-figure stand of the summer against Surrey at Kennington. Palmer declared first thing on Thursday morning and Leicestershire's 314 was then the highest score by any visiting side. Surrey, thanks to centuries by Stewart and Constable, took control. The pitch, which at first proved fast, became dusty on the third day when Eric Bedser seized the chance to accomplish the best bowling performance of his career with 7-33. Surridge distinguished himself by taking seven catches, most of them brilliant. The batsmen hurried to the crease and by consistent forcing cricket, Surrey gained their thirteenth Championship victory by a comfortable margin of five wickets but with only ten minutes left of the extra half-hour.

Still at the Oval, Kent triumphed in one of the most dramatic finishes of the season, winning by 13 runs and avenging their crushing defeat by the champions the previous week. Surrey seemed certain of victory with Barrington and Pratt batting comfortably and requiring just 29 runs with six wickets left to fall. Then Allan, who had bowled his left-arm slows with persistent accuracy on a pitch giving no help, dismissed Pratt and for the second time in the match Surrey collapsed in astonishing fashion. Reckless strokes accounted for McIntyre, Laker and Surridge; Cox was out first ball. Barrington, having batted excellently for two-and-a-quarter hours, then fell in trying to score the single needed to keep the bowling. The last six wickets went down in twenty minutes, Allan claiming four of them in fifteen deliveries. Kent batted poorly on the first day when, in ideal conditions, Pettiford alone offered much resistance to Surrey's weakened attack. Surrey appeared to be heading for a useful lead when Wright and Allan caused the first collapse, the score moving from 123/3 to 132/9 in half an hour. Kent reached 91/5 before a cloudburst ended play on the second evening and the following morning Laker and Bedser made full use of the rain-affected turf. When this dried out, Surrey appeared to have a simple task but they were unable to capitalise.

Haydn Davies captained an all-professional side of Welshmen for the first time in Glamorgan history in the match against Surrey but they were scarcely a match for the Champions at Swansea, who gained a fairly easy victory in two days. Laker's splendid all-round form provided the chief feature of the match. Besides taking 10-121, he scored 53 through

A ball is glanced fine and evades Surridge in the Surrey leg-trap.

bold hitting. Eric Bedser and Barrington also batted well for Surrey but apart from Parkhouse and Haydn Davies, Glamorgan's batsmen were disappointing.

Moving to Worcester, Surrey achieved another comfortable win by eight wickets. Surrey were put on the right path by Stewart and Constable, whose second-wicket stand realised 104 in eighty minutes. Constable completed his first century of the season before his first mistake, a mistimed hook, cost him his wicket. The Surrey bowlers, Alec Bedser and Laker in particular, built on the solid foundations laid by the batsmen. On the second day they took seventeen wickets and when stumps were drawn Worcestershire still needed two runs to avoid an innings defeat.

Their successes against Glamorgan and Worcestershire had been achieved whilst four players, May, Lock, McIntyre and Loader, were appearing for England in a Test match. Lock and Loader returned to the side at Coventry where Warwickshire won by 131 runs in a game notable for a fine hundred by their left-hander, Hitchcock. With a total of 134/3 they were well placed at lunch on the first day but Surrey wrested the initiative after the break when Laker, switching ends, took five of the last seven wickets for 32. Surrey lost half their side for 58 to the fast bowling of Thompson and Bannister before Barrington and Swetman staged a partial recovery. Warwickshire, leading by 56, might not have established such a strong position but for a glorious exhibition of strokes by Hitchcock in his unbeaten 123. Surrey had in their grasp the chance of obtaining the 307 needed for victory so long as Barrington remained but when he was sixth out at 145, after a stay of two hours, all hope disappeared.

Surrey returned to winning ways as they entertained Nottinghamshire at the Oval over the Bank Holiday. The match took a sensational turn late on the second day when Nottinghamshire batted a second time 43 runs in arrears. They went in at 5.25 p.m.; one hour later six wickets were down for 25 and Laker's analysis read: 6-5-1-4. No one anticipated the collapse and, well as Laker bowled on a dusty pitch, he owed much of his success that day to some magnificent fielding. In fact, a wonderful left-handed catch to dismiss Giles by Stewart at silly mid-on, only eight yards from the bat, began the trouble for Nottinghamshire. Lock and Surridge also made brilliant catches. Surridge claimed the extra half-hour but Kelly, despite an injured left arm, stayed forty minutes. Close of play found Nottinghamshire with only one wicket left, their score being 30/9. Next morning just seven minutes were needed with Lock and Laker each bowling one more maiden over before Surridge caught his rival captain, Jepson, splendidly at slip.

Surrey then triumphed over Lancashire at Old Trafford by seven wickets. Again they were indebted to the intelligent bowling of Lock. In a spell on the first day he took 6-10 after Ikin, with his second century of the season, helped Lancashire to score 188/2 by tea. On a good pitch, Lock kept a nagging length and was aided by alert fielding close to the wicket. Despite attractive batting by Barrington and a breezy innings by Laker, Surrey conceded first-innings points by 28 runs. Lock again proved troublesome to Lancashire in their second innings, when he completed a match analysis of 13-130, and Surrey had plenty of time in which to score the 154 required to win.

Middlesex were beaten at the Oval by 39 runs. After they had won the toss for only the fourth time in twenty-one Championship matches, Surrey lost four wickets for six runs against some admirable bowling by Warr and Moss, who exploited a green pitch and heavy atmosphere. Surrey fought back and a sixth-wicket stand of 92 by Barrington and Swetman gave them a sporting chance on a pitch that turned in favour of the spin bowlers on the second day. Lock revelled in the conditions, taking 13 wickets for the second successive match, but Dewes proved to be in his best form and he carried his bat for 101 in an innings lasting four hours. Then Stewart showed the same determination for Surrey, who left Middlesex to make 166. Whereas Laker, who was troubled with a sore spinning figure, accomplished little, Lock again thwarted Middlesex; the turning-point came when he held a fierce return catch from Dewes, who was third out at 64.

Four away matches then followed. The Somerset batsmen were no match for Surrey's bowlers on a spiteful pitch at Weston-super-Mare. Surrey did well to score 227 but they owed most to May who gave a delightful display against the lifting and turning ball. Then came a dramatic dénouement, Somerset found Lock and Alec Bedser almost unplayable and were dismissed for 36, the lowest total of the season. Lock did the hat-trick for the first time in his career when he dismissed McMahon and Lobb at the end of the first innings and Angell with his first ball of the second when Somerset followed-on 191 behind. Only an hour-and-a-quarter was needed on the second day, after Lock and Alec Bedser again routed the home county. Lock took 10-54 in the match and Alec Bedser 9-46.

Gloucestershire put up a good fight before going down to the Champions at Cheltenham by 43 runs. The pitch was always difficult but Surrey, after losing half their side for 39, fought back through a hard-hitting innings by Cox. He took 24 off one over from Wells and altogether he made 57 in fifty-five minutes. Despite a steady innings by

Young, Gloucestershire also collapsed. Although set the reasonable task of scoring 123 on a pitch playing a little easier, Gloucestershire failed in face of determined bowling and brilliant catching. In the absence of Laker, Clark bowled his off-breaks effectively and Alec Bedser, who bowled unchanged, also did extremely well.

Two fine innings by Arnold and a splendid all-round performance by Tribe were mainly responsible for Northamptonshire's victory over the champions at Northampton. Surrey's chances of a first-innings lead seemed slender when Brookes and Arnold took Northamptonshire's first-wicket stand to 122. Devastating bowling by Loader and Cox brought such a collapse that Surrey led by 29. Tribe took 6-66 in their second innings. Then, with Northamptonshire needing 202 to win, he shared stands of 105 with Arnold and 60 with Broderick. Owing to the final Test being played at the Oval, Surrey were without May, Laker and Lock.

Surrey were still not sure of the Championship as Yorkshire were at their heels all the time and Surrey went to Lord's conscious of the responsibilities that lay ahead. In the end they won comfortably by nine wickets. Surrey were much stronger in all facets of the game and once more Lock proved a match-winning bowler. He only decided to play at the last minute because a sore spinning finger had been troublesome. A crowd of 20,000 saw him take 5-62 on Saturday when Middlesex collapsed after a good innings from Delisle. Their last five wickets fell for just 18 runs. Barrington and Eric Bedser shared a stand of 114 and with Stewart also showing fine form, Surrey led by 84. On a dusty pitch, Middlesex broke down again and Lock made his match record 9-108. Surrey required only 32 to win.

Back at the Oval against Sussex, Surrey were in serious danger at the end of the first day but they recovered to win the game in emphatic style and their victory made certain of retaining the Championship. Sussex lost four wickets for 75 at the start, but recovered through resolute batting by Parks, Suttle, Cox and Thompson. Before the close, four Surrey wickets fell for 32 but the following day Surrey took command. Constable, batting for four hours, played a vital part in the recovery and Barrington, McIntyre and Laker supported him well. McIntyre hit tremendously hard and his 81 included fourteen boundaries. Against a tiring attack Laker and Surridge added 68 in fifty minutes. Two spectacular slip catches by May off Alec Bedser started the Sussex breakdown when they went in 98 behind. On a worn pitch, Alec Bedser and Lock bowled so effectively that on the last morning Sussex lost their last eight wickets in ninety-five minutes for 78.

By beating Surrey at Bournemouth, Hampshire gained the points that assured them finishing higher in the Championship than ever before in their history; Hampshire took full advantage of an ideal batting pitch. Gray and Marshall began with a partnership of 102 in less than an hour and a half. Subsequently Horton stayed three hours forty minutes while Hampshire established a commanding position. Surrey were in danger of having to follow-on but an eighth wicket stand of 69 in an hour and a quarter between Laker and Lock saved them from this indignity. Hampshire scored at a brisk rate and set Surrey to get 304 in four hours. Pratt and Stewart kept the Champions ahead of the clock but at 56 Rogers ran out Stewart from mid-wicket and thereafter the only issue was whether Surrey would be dismissed in the time available. Sainsbury, the young left-arm slow bowler, in taking four wickets in six overs after tea at a cost of 13 runs, hastened Surrey's downfall.

Surrey completed their Championship programme against Derbyshire, with three of their younger members, Pratt, Stewart and Barrington, batting well to bring about victory within two days. Previously, the game ran very much to form with each side stronger in bowling and fielding than in batting. Smith, the young off-spinner, helped Derbyshire to pass 100 by hitting 22 in the last-wicket stand of 32, the best partnership of the innings. Only Willett, who in his first game showed great promise, and Laker reached double figures for Surrey. They hit 63 out of a total of 101. Derbyshire collapsed in their second innings against the fast bowling of Surridge. The Surrey captain took 6-56 runs, his best figures of the summer.

Peter May again headed the averages but scored only 1,320 runs for Surrey at 45.51. Barrington scored 1,418 runs at 36.33, Constable

1,208 at 25.16 and Stewart 1,085 at 29.32. Interestingly, McIntyre just failed to reach 1,000 runs scoring 920 runs at 26.28. Tony Lock was streets ahead in the bowling figures taking 183 wickets at 12.22 but was well supported by Alec Bedser with 131 at 17.61, Laker 124 at 17.63 and Loader with 88 at 14.79. Surrey held 383 catches during the season, with three members of the side holding over 50 catches each.

FOURTEEN

1956

Surrey, enthusiastically led by Stuart Surridge and possessing an attack of international class in the Bedser twins, Loader, Laker and Lock, carried off the Championship for the fifth successive year, an achievement without parallel. Moreover, they accomplished another feat that had not been performed for forty-four years, as in the middle of May they defeated the Australians at the Oval by ten wickets. They retained the title on 31 August, with the abandonment of their match with Lancashire, in which not a ball could be bowled after tea on the first afternoon. The victory of the weather was an appropriate enough climax to one of the most miserable summers in living memory.

There was no doubt that once again Surrey were the best-equipped side in the Championship. During their five triumphant years under Surridge they have been, perhaps, fortunate in being able to call on the same nucleus of players. Looking at the names of the men who took Surrey to the top in 1952, one finds that the only two notable personalities who had passed from the ranks were Laurie Fishlock and Jack Parker. Throughout the winning run of five Championship titles, the county have been geared into action by the motivational power of Surridge, who moved into retirement with a most remarkable personal record. Like A.B. Sellers, who led Yorkshire in their invincible pre-war period, Surridge inspired his men to a very high standard of fielding in which he himself set the prime example. In turn, Yorkshire and Surrey had shown that a first-rate bowling combination supported by brilliant

The Surrey team of 1956, left to right, back row: B. Constable, D.G.W. Fletcher, G.A.R. Lock, P.J. Loader, K.F. Barrington, M.J. Stewart. Front row: E.A. Bedser, A.V. Bedser, W.S. Surridge, P.B.H. May, A.J.W. McIntyre, J.C. Laker..

fielding, especially close to the batsman, were essential components of a winning team.

Compared with 1955, when they boasted a record number of points by reaching 284, Surrey could show no more than 200 in 1956, a drop largely owing to the abnormally wet weather. Rain caused eight of their Championship games to be left drawn, whereas during the previous season every match was brought to a definite conclusion.

Although Surrey were always in a challenging position, they did not head the Championship table until the first week of July and then their tenure was insecure, for Lancashire mostly led the way in June and July. Subsequently, four successive wins against Essex, Middlesex (twice) and Sussex in August carried Surrey ahead and they had to be thankful that they had some games in hand for owing to the weather, none of their last five Championship matches produced a definite result.

With the turf at the Oval giving much more help in recent years to bowlers compared with the days when only interests of batsmen received attention, Surrey again thrived on a minimum quantity of runs. In all of their 36 first-class matches they reached 300 only six times, their highest total being 404/4 declared against Kent at Blackheath. On that occasion Clark made 190 not out, then the best of his career, which he beat by a single in the very next match, against Gloucestershire, at the Oval. The return to form of Clark was most welcome. Owing to hip trouble, he made only 596 runs in the Championship in 1955; now he headed the batting with 1,325, average 34.86. Both Stewart and Barrington took some time to find their form and consequently were left out of the side, but each returned to a permanent place.

To Peter May, the vice-captain, the season brought mixed fortunes. As England captain for the second year, May carried a heavy responsibility to his country and in the five Tests he made 453 runs in seven innings, averaging 90.60, a truly magnificent performance, but for Surrey he shed some of that lustre. His Championship return fell from 41.86 to 32.48, yet he scored over 1,000 runs for Surrey alone. There was no decline in May's batting; rather did he emphasise his dependability on the big occasion.

The contribution of Jim Laker to Surrey's fifth Championship was relatively small. He appeared in only 13 inter-county matches and his wickets numbered 57 against 117 in 1955. He fared better against the Australians than the English counties, for in seven matches against the touring team he took 63 wickets, including 46 in Tests. Rain ruined his benefit match against Yorkshire, but the public regarded him as a national hero and contributed generously.

Whereas Lock twice saw Laker take all ten wickets against the Australians, he himself achieved the performance against Kent at Blackheath when Laker was resting. A dynamic cricketer, Lock headed the Surrey Championship bowling with 117 wickets, average 10.46, figures which tell eloquently of his ability, for he appeared in only 17 matches. Loader, with 102 wickets, and Alec Bedser, with 83, were a grand opening pair, and Eric Bedser proved an invaluable all-rounder. In all matches he scored 804 runs and took 92 wickets and he was

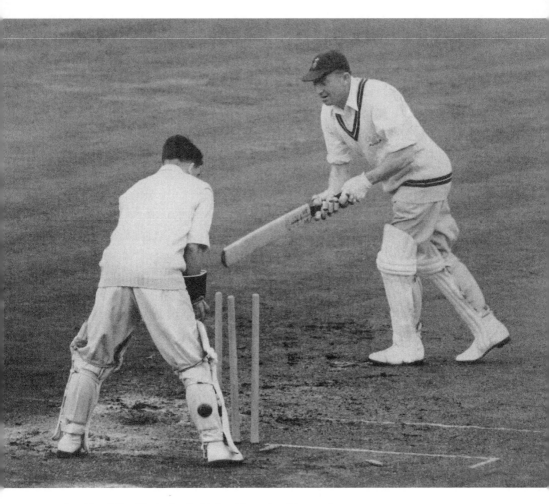

Surridge fails with the bat in his last Championship match.

most unfortunate that rain robbed him of the chance of accomplishing the double. Surridge expressed the opinion that, without Eric Bedser, Surrey might not have retained the Championship. Even when Laker and Lock were present, Bedser was still a prominent member of the attack.

A damaged hand kept McIntyre out for half the season, during which time his fearless batting was badly missed. His aggregate fell by over 700, but on his return he kept wicket as well as ever and he attended the final Test as deputy to Godfrey Evans.

The first Championship match of the season against Derbyshire at the Oval was drawn. Most of the excitement came on the last day when Derbyshire wanted 232 in four hours and twenty minutes. Apart from Lee who drove strongly, the early batsmen made slow progress. Kelly, for example, took one hour forty minutes over 23. Lock bowled and fielded magnificently. With twenty minutes left and the total 201/6, Loader took the new ball and Surrey proceeded to dismiss Gladwin, Rhodes and Jackson. Two balls remained when the last man, Smith, appeared and he coolly applied the dead bat to both. So for the first time after a run of forty-two consecutive matches Surrey were engaged in a draw. For most of the game Derbyshire adopted a negative attitude; only 782 runs were scored in eighteen hours. On the first day, when Surrey won the toss, their first seven wickets fell for 99 but May showed his own high class and Surridge, paying no respect to leg theory, hit twelve fours in his dashing unbeaten 70, which he made in 100 minutes.

Surridge did not play in the next match against Northamptonshire at the Oval, who beat Surrey by seven wickets. But at Cardiff Arms Park, Surrey won their first match of the season against Glamorgan by 168 runs. On a lively pitch, bowling with his old fire and zest, Alec Bedser took seven wickets in each innings for the modest cost of 69 runs. Shepherd, for Glamorgan, proved almost as successful with off-cutters, sending back twelve men but a useful opening stand by Fletcher and Clark helped Surrey to a first-innings lead of 62. A forceful fifth-wicket partnership of 95 in as many minutes by Barrington and Pratt in the second innings led to Glamorgan being set 273 to win, a task well beyond their powers.

After their famous win over the Australians as described in the next chapter, Surrey travelled to Trent Bridge for their usual Whitsun fixture Nottinghamshire, who won by 187 runs on turf which took spin from the start. Slow bowlers dominated the game to such an extent that thirty-eight of the forty wickets fell to them. Surprisingly, Laker and Lock proved less effective than Nottinghamshire's pair, Smales and Dooland, though Laker was troubled at first by a sore finger. The inclusion of a left-handed batsman might have helped Surrey, for Nottinghamshire's batting was carried in the first innings by Poole and in the second by Stocks. Jepson, a right-hander, also played an invaluable

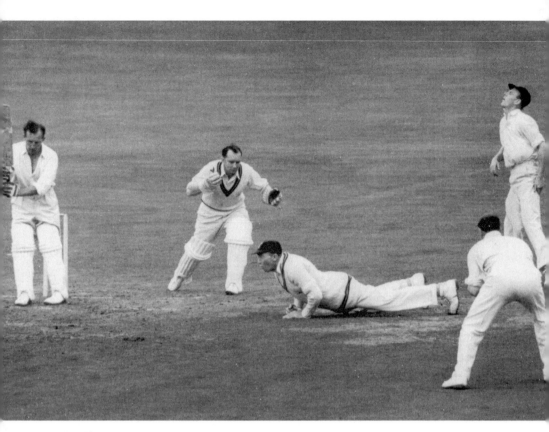

Surridge just misses an opportunity.

part in checking Lock on the first day, with all but two of his runs coming from boundaries. Of the Surrey batsmen, May alone displayed any ability to overcome the conditions.

Surrey returned to their winning ways at Leicester but were again without Surridge. Surrey scored 238 in their first innings and Leicestershire came pretty close to a first-innings lead, falling just short of Surrey's total. Surrey's second innings was declared at 2 p.m. on the third day and Leicestershire were promptly shot out for 78. The match was all over before half-past four. At the Wagon Works Ground in Gloucester, the home team triumphed over the Champions by ten runs. Once again, off-spin bowling decided the match. Surrey had plenty of time to make 150 for victory but their batsmen were puzzled by Mortimore who appropriately finished the game by holding a return catch. Gloucestershire, lacking the services of Graveney, Milton and Young, fell to the wiles of Laker and Lock when put in on a drying pitch but their spin bowlers dismissed Surrey for a moderate score. Then came a splendid home recovery inspired by the soundness of Emmett and forcefulness of Crapp and Nicholls. Surrey, without loss, hit off fourteen of the runs wanted in the last half-hour of the second day, but after being 83/4 they were beaten in an exciting finish.

Surridge was not deterred on coming back to the Oval. He won the toss and put Leicestershire in on a pitch affected by rain the previous day. The first innings ended in an hour and forty minutes. Alec Bedser and Lock proved altogether too much for timid batsmen. Thanks to a stand of 72 by May and Stewart and brisk driving by Eric Bedser, Surrey were able to declare 103 ahead. Leicestershire did better at the second attempt and Hallam, who gave one difficult chance, in partnership with Palmer, added 76. Good fielding, in which May played a leading part, caused another collapse despite a careful stand of 50 by Smithson and Smith. Surrey, needing 119, lost two wickets for 57 but Fletcher, cautiously, and May, in his best form, finished the light task.

At the Oval, Somerset were beaten by an innings and nine runs with twenty minutes to spare. The honours of the match went to Peter Wight who, on a rain-affected pitch, scored 62 out of Somerset's first innings of 159 and 128 out of 196 in the second. He batted for eight hours altogether without being dismissed, showing extraordinary calm in difficult circumstances. Surrey were fortunate to bat on a firm pitch and given a sound start by Fletcher and Clark they shaped the innings authoritatively, but against some accurate slow left-arm bowling by McMahon, their former colleague, they did not display much freedom in strokeplay until 6 p.m. Surridge hit out boldly, making 52 out of 75 in half an hour. The value of his enterprise was emphasised when Surrey were able to enforce the follow-on and press home their advantage thanks to some keen bowling, especially by Loader who took ten wickets in the match.

The match against Hampshire at Portsmouth was a sad example of Surrey batting failures and they lost by 28 runs. On a rain-affected pitch batsmen were always at a disadvantage, and on the second day 25 wickets fell for 230 runs. Loader and Alec Bedser began the batsmen's troubles by taking the last five Hampshire wickets in less than an hour for 33 runs. Fletcher and Clark gave Surrey a fine start but Burden, with off-breaks, and Sainsbury, with skilful left-arm deliveries, dismissed the rest of the side in fifty-five minutes for the addition of 36 runs. The lively pace of Loader and Alec Bedser disposed of Hampshire before the close and Surrey began the third day requiring 137 to win. They looked well placed with the total at 48/1 but two fine catches close to the wicket by Eagar swung the game in Hampshire's favour. Marshall, pitching his off-breaks accurately, prevented Surrey from regaining the initiative.

Surrey won their match against Yorkshire at the Oval with ten minutes to spare but from the financial aspect Laker's benefit match was a tragedy. Rain prevented any cricket on the first day and the weather remained so dull and doubtful that less than 10,000 people saw the game which was completed in two days and provided an exciting finish. Watson, the Yorkshire captain, asked Surrey to bat on a soft pitch. The bowlers always held the upper hand with Appleyard (9-59) and Lock (9-71) the outstanding performers. After Yorkshire had gained a lead of 12 runs, Clark played the most important innings and for the first time in his career he carried his bat. Despite this effort, Yorkshire were left to make 124 in two hours and twenty minutes and possessed a fine chance of victory. They began slowly, scoring only 25 in fifty minutes before tea for the loss of Illingworth. Then came a stand of 49 by left-handers Close and Wilson and Yorkshire were on good terms with the clock, but they became reckless and mistakes led to Surrey snatching a victory that an hour earlier scarcely seemed possible.

In a close fixture at Guildford the last Hampshire wicket fell five minutes from time. Surrey, without five of their regular team, were tied to defence on the first day. Fletcher, in particular, set himself up to occupy the crease and stayed there for nearly five hours. Shackleton took 5-27 in twelve overs after tea. Hampshire began badly, but gained the lead with the last pair together, as Sainsbury skilfully 'farmed' the bowling. Stewart and Barrington each hit their first hundred of the summer when Surrey batted again and Hampshire were set to get 239 at 78 runs an hour. They scored 100 in eighty minutes but once the dashing Marshall departed the crease, the initiative swung to Surrey

Stuart Surridge
with a future
Surrey captain
– Micky Stewart.

and Alec Bedser finished the game with the new ball as Surrey won
by 37 runs.

Kent were beaten by eight wickets at the Oval. The winning
run came from a boundary overthrow off the last ball of the extra
half-hour on the second day. Lock, returning to the Surrey side
after internal trouble, and Loader caused a collapse in Kent's first
innings after the early batsmen had shown considerable enterprise.
Surrey owed their lead of 78 mainly to May who, overcoming early
uncertainty, mastered some accurate spin bowling by Wright and
Page. Batting for four hours, May hit seven boundaries in his first
hundred of the season. Showers followed by sunshine provided an
ideal pitch for Lock and Laker when Kent batted again and they were

dismissed in one hundred minutes. This left Surrey to make only 21, a feat accomplished in ten minutes.

A rare second defeat by Northamptonshire, who won by seven wickets, followed at Northampton. As in the first match at the Oval, it was the spin bowlers, Manning and Tribe, who made the most important contribution to their victory. Barrington dominated a Surrey innings which was colourless until Laker hit 43 in 28 minutes. Northamptonshire scored more briskly and the lead was virtually assured by a third-wicket stand of 112 by Livingston and Barrick. When Surrey batted the last seven wickets fell for 50 runs. Northamptonshire easily hit off the runs needed for victory.

Kent were completely outplayed by Surrey for the second time in a week, the match being notable for the bowling of Lock and the batting exploits of Clark and May. In excellent conditions Clark batted masterfully on the first day in hitting 191, the highest score of his career. May batted far more convincingly than when scoring a century against Kent the previous week; much of his strokeplay being superb. Weekend rain added to Kent's plight and on the Monday, when Surridge declared first thing, Lock received enough help from the turf to shatter Kent's moderate batting. Kent scored only 101 in their first innings and followed-on. By the close of the second day Lock was in sight of all ten wickets for the first time and he achieved it the following morning by dismissing the last four batsmen without conceding a run. His 16-83 made his figures for the two games against Kent 26-143.

At the Oval, rain played a big part in the match against Gloucestershire for it induced Emmett to send Surrey in to bat and it ended cricket at 2.50 p.m. on the last day. Any hopes that Gloucestershire's venture might succeed were destroyed by Clark, who completed another impressive century, making 190. Gloucestershire began disastrously but careful play by Young and Graveney saw 145 put on in three hours. Crapp then assisted Young and added 128. After Young left there came a collapse. Surrey led by 58 and free hitting brought 153 runs in a hundred minutes but rain checked their efforts to force a win.

We then come to one of the most important matches played in the five triumphant years against Yorkshire at Bramall Lane as Surrey completed their first double over Yorkshire for thirty-six years. They triumphed dramatically on the last day when Yorkshire looked set for victory. Sent in to bat, Surrey began well with Stewart and Barrington putting on 73 for the second wicket. The fourth wicket fell at 103 and then came complete collapse, the last six wickets falling in forty minutes for 25. Illingworth took three wickets in four balls during one over. Wilson and Close then batted well for Yorkshire who led on the first innings by 61. May and Barrington added 94 for the third Surrey wicket but most of the other batsmen were in trouble and Yorkshire needed only 97 to win. They were 30/2 overnight and began the last day needing 67. They gave a disappointing display against accurate bowling on a not-too-difficult pitch and lost their remaining eight wickets in two-and-a-quarter hours for 52. Lock took five of the last six wickets in eleven overs for just 11 runs.

At this stage of the season Lancashire, having played two more games, led Surrey in the Championship by 12 points. Therefore, the win over Yorkshire was the pivotal moment of the year. At Hastings the Champions took the initiative against Sussex on the opening day when they built up a steady, substantial total against some accurate bowling. A third-wicket stand of 157 by Barrington and Constable was followed by a collapse before some powerful hitting by Surridge enabled him to declare. Sussex had a strange opening pair of batsmen in Potter and Webb but along with the left-handed Smith they profited and reached 200/4 before the pace of Loader combined with the leg-breaks of David Pratt caused a complete collapse. Again the early Surrey batsmen did well and though Marlar later proved effective, Surridge again closed the innings. Sussex wanted 274 in just under three-and-a-half hours and made a gallant attempt to hit off the runs. Smith and Parks put on 75 in less than an hour but in the end the Bedser twins bowled Surrey to victory.

Essex were beaten at the Oval by 109 runs. Once again bowling strength pulled them through and pace, swerve and spin were all effective against uncertain opponents. Essex began well enough by dismissing Surrey before tea but the visitors who had been checked by the soundness of Stewart and enterprising strokeplay of Surridge had little answer to the speed and accuracy of Loader. Despite good efforts by Dodds and Insole, who shared in a century stand after three wickets fell for six runs, Essex were unable to cope with Loader who took 8-50 in an innings of 150. Barrington, Constable and the enthusiastic Surridge played the biggest parts in increasing Surrey's advantage to 255 but Essex, even with five-and-a-half hours to get the runs, never looked capable of completing the task. The Surrey captain, for the last innings, put his faith in swerve and spin and the Bedser twins and David Pratt justified his policy.

From the moment Surridge decided to put Nottinghamshire in to bat at the Oval, little went right for Surrey. The pitch dried slowly and while it played easily, Giles and Winfield were able to give Nottinghamshire a sound start, scoring 88 together. Although conditions became more difficult as the day progressed Dooland and Walker ensured a respectable total during a seventh-wicket partnership of 50. After a lost second day through rain, Surrey found themselves on spiteful turf and were dismissed in two hours and twenty minutes. Following-on 157 behind, Surrey again lost wickets cheaply but this time a capable display by Barrington dispelled any thoughts of an outright success for Nottinghamshire.

The win over Essex at Clacton-on-Sea was achieved in the nick of time. A superb 166 by Stewart, his highest score in first-class cricket, and deadly bowling by Lock and Loader were the decisive factors. Stewart, who batted for five hours, drove and hooked faultlessly. Insole twice batted soundly but Lock took five wickets in each innings. Needing just 60 to win, Surrey had a fright in the second innings, losing half their wickets for 37 before McIntyre made the winning hit as heavy rain started. The game attracted a record attendance to the ground on which a Championship match was first played twenty-five years previously in 1931.

Two wins followed at the Oval where Middlesex and Sussex were the visitors. A notable spell of fast-medium bowling by Loader in the Middlesex match and an innings of technical skill and immense concentration by Bill Edrich provided features of an intriguing struggle. Loader, taking advantage of an unusually 'green' pitch before lunch, took six of the first seven wickets at a personal cost of 12 runs. While much of their batting was unimpressive, Surrey established a commanding position. Middlesex, who struggled to 37/4, appeared unlikely to clear arrears of 107 but Edrich, in demonstrating how the

Arriving home on day of retirement – met by wife Betty and son, Stuart.

turning ball should be played found an excellent partner in Bennett. The pair added 60 runs and Edrich stayed four-and-a-quarter hours while making 82 out of 138. Despite his brave performance, Surrey made light of their task of scoring 82 and lost just three wickets. Seven wickets was also the margin of victory over Sussex where the failure of the late-order batsmen to consolidate a sound start in each innings contributed to their downfall. The spin of Lock and Eric Bedser caused these rapid deteriorations on a pitch showing signs of dust surprisingly early in the match. A dropped catch when seven wickets were down for 122 helped Surrey to gain a lead of 21. Laker, the fortunate batsman, hit lustily in partnership with McIntyre and 55 runs were added in twenty-five minutes. Sussex looked to be moving to a sound position during a stand of 87 between Doggart and Suttle but once again Lock and Eric Bedser hastened the end of the innings. Stewart and Constable batted so attractively that Surrey obtained the 104 runs needed with the minimum of trouble.

The winning streak continued as they moved to Lord's for the return match with Middlesex. On a pitch always receptive to spin Titmus and Lock accomplished splendid performances. Titmus also made 50, the best score of the match, but his all-round efforts – he also took 14-110 –failed to bring success. Play did not start until 1 p.m. on the first day. Surrey struggled throughout the innings but took four Middlesex wickets for 31 before the close. The steady succession of dismissals continued on Monday and Surrey contrived to lead by 50. Titmus was to the fore and eventually Middlesex were set 209 to win, Middlesex collapsed in the face of the inestimable Lock, who took 12-75 in the game.

At Derby a Surrey side without the likes of May, Laker, Lock and McIntyre – who were required at the Oval Test – fought hard but could not gain any points. They lost five first innings wickets for 44 runs but Constable batted bravely and, with good support from Swetman and Pratt, compiled a respectable score. Lee and Kelly gave Derbyshire a good start and despite good sustained pace bowling by Loader, Derbyshire gained the lead. Stewart completed a hundred before Surridge declared and left Derbyshire to make 142 in two hours. Derbyshire declined to accept this sporting challenge, Kelly in particular batting dourly.

At Edgbaston so much time was lost because of rain that obtaining first-innings points was the only issue at stake. The first day's play was restricted to two hours, and none was possible on the second day. On the last morning, Warwickshire lost their eight remaining wickets for 53 in the face of the bowling of Eric Bedser and Loader. Surrey, with ample time, made sure of the points with Stewart and Fletcher adding 124 for the second wicket.

The eagerly awaited meeting of Lancashire and Surrey at Old Trafford, chief contenders for the Championship practically all the summer, ended on a most disappointing note. After Lancashire had promised to keep alive their slender hopes of wresting the title from their rivals by dismissing Surrey for 96, heavy rain washed out play on the last two days. Surrey, sent in to bat on a pitch already made soft by repeated storms, were always struggling. Tattersall made the most of the conditions and his analysis 6-32 in twenty-one overs represented an intelligent and skilful display of off-spin bowling. Lancashire reached 40 for the loss of Wharton and Geoff Edrich before torrential rain at tea made its untimely intervention.

Surrey were now champions yet again but the season finished with a very damp air. The match at Worcester fizzled out in a draw and the final match against Warwickshire at the Oval was abandoned without a ball being bowled.

The season's batting averages were headed by Micky Stewart with 1,537 runs at 34.15, with Clark scoring a few more runs with 1,561 at 33.21. Barrington scored 1,250 runs, Constable 1,188 and May 1,178. Lock again headed the bowling list with 138 wickets, Loader had 122, Alec Bedser 96, Eric Bedser 92 and Laker 84.

FIFTEEN

Surrey Beat the Australians

It can be said that one of the proudest moments in Stuart Surridge's reign as Surrey captain came on Friday 18 May 1956 when his beloved county defeated the Australian touring team. Surrey became the first county team for forty-four years to triumph over an Australian team.

Winning the toss appeared to give the Australians a considerable advantage and Burke and McDonald emphasised this view while scoring 62 in ninety-five minutes. McDonald, though enjoying two 'lives', brought off many good strokes during a stay of three hours and thirty-five minutes and he fell only 11 runs short of his second century in successive innings. When he was taken at the wicket the total stood at 151/4 but Laker so bamboozled the Aussies that five more batsmen were dismissed while the total rose by just 48. Of these runs twelve, including a drive for six, were hit by Davidson in one over from Laker and sixteen came in three strokes by Crawford at the same bowler's expense. Fortunately for the Australians, Miller, in facing as much of the bowling as possible, scored briskly after a careful start and he and Wilson put on 42 for the last wicket. Even so, Laker maintained a splendid length in a spell of four and a quarter hours, broken only by the lunch and tea intervals. He exploited the dry pitch so skilfully that he came out with the analysis 46-18-88-10.

Jim Laker recalled in his book *A Spell from Laker*:

I certainly have Stuart Surridge to thank on the occasion of my all ten Australian wickets for Surrey in 1956. Feeling far from 100 per cent fit when I arrived at the Oval that morning due to a very rough night with two sick children, I was hoping that he would bat first on a pretty good wicket. It was not to be, and shortly I was in the middle of a long yet most productive spell. An unbroken session of thirty overs had brought me the first six Australian wickets, by which time I suggested to Stuart that I was just about on my knees and we had sufficiently good bowlers to polish off the remaining Australians. He would have none of it, and over the next hour and a half he cajoled and persuaded me to keep having another couple of overs. Finally after forty-six overs I had all ten wickets to my name and the most delighted person at the Oval was the Surrey captain.

In the hope that he might achieve similar success, Ian Johnson kept himself on for most of the Surrey first innings but though he flighted the ball well, his off-breaks caused nothing like the same trouble. Apart from three overs by the fast bowlers, the Australian attack remained in the hands of the spin bowlers throughout, a policy which not only failed to bring the desired results, but came in for much criticism.

Still, Surrey did not find run-getting an easy matter for a long time, though Fletcher drove hard during an opening stand with Clark which realised 53. Clark stayed while another 59 runs were added, giving no chance during two hours and ten minutes. Constable, cautious at first, gradually developed more freedom but wickets fell steadily and Surrey were down to 221/6. Then Laker attacked the bowling, he helped himself to sixteen, including a drive for six and two fours, in an over from Johnson, and altogether hit 43 out of 57 added by the seventh-wicket partnership in thirty-nine minutes, taking Surrey ahead. Constable's long stay ended with a return catch after he had batted for four hours and thirty-five minutes. Without making a serious mistake, he hit seven fours in a most valuable innings. To add the icing to the cake, Surridge and Loader put on 34 for the last wicket.

Three overs by the opening Surrey bowlers at the end of the second day did not yield a run nor a wicket; next morning Surridge reverted

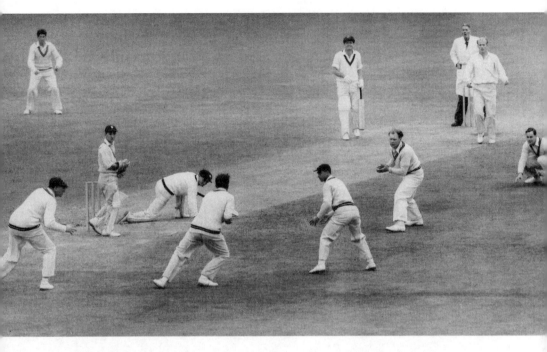

Maddocks caught by Laker off Lock in second innings. Surrey players (left to right): Barrington, Surridge, Swetman, Laker, Fletcher, Cox, May and Lock. Other batsman is Mackay. (Photograph from Roger Mann Collection)

to an all-spin attack. For a time matters went well enough with the Australians and an opening stand of 56 in ninety-five minutes by Burke and McDonald seemed to have made them reasonably safe from defeat. Then the course of the game changed completely, for Lock, now able to make the ball turn quickly and occasionally get up awkwardly from a dusty pitch, caused such a breakdown that in a further ninety-five minutes the innings was all over for another 51 runs. Lock, who took the first six wickets at a cost of 40 runs, finished with an analysis of 7-49 in marked contrast to his 0-100 in the first innings. He achieved all of his success from the Pavilion End, from which Laker had bowled in the first innings in a spell of 23.1 overs, 6 maidens, for 36 runs. He owed something to smart fielding, as the catch taken by May at slip to dismiss Davidson was first-rate. Surrey required only 20 runs to win, but Lindwall and Crawford bowled so fast and accurately that they took fifty-five minutes to accomplish the task.

Stuart Surridge being presented with an Australian baggy green cap by their captain, Ian
Johnson. Surridge had lead Surrey to victory against the tourists at the Oval.

The last time that Surrey had beaten the Australian touring team was
way back in 1912. Two of the participants in that match were at the Oval to
see Surrey's triumph in 1956. Sir Jack Hobbs was in the committee room
and Herbert Strudwick, who had kept wicket in the 1912 match, was there
too. He was in the scorer's box as official Surrey scorer. Back in 1912 the
win had come by 21 runs in a surprise finish. The remainder of the team
in that match were: Tom Hayward, E.G. Hayes, Andy Ducat, M.C. Bird,
Bobby Abel, E.B. Myers, Bill Hitch, W.C. Smith and T. Rushby.

When the players had left the field Johnson's first action was to take
his familiar green cap to Surrey's captain, Stuart Surridge, and present it

to him with a 'well done'. In a later interview Johnson said: 'Surrey fully deserved their win. We congratulate them. Laker and Lock bowled so well and were so supported by a very good fielding side.' Johnson was then asked how many caps he brought with him? 'Two' he replied, and grinning broadly added: 'I will not have any occasion to give the other one away.'

A happy Surridge was asked if he had handed over his cap to Johnson. 'Mine is very old and tattered,' he said. 'And anyway, it's a lucky hat.' The last county to have beaten the Australians was Hampshire. In the same 1912 season, Surrey, Lancashire (twice) and Nottinghamshire also beat the tourists.

Surridge thought Johnson a fine sporting captain and at the time he said the whole Australian team took their medicine like real sportsmen. The cap remained a treasure among the many souvenirs in the Surridge home at Wandsworth. Ironically, at a later date Surridge was asked to lend the cap out for a special function and being the generous man he was agreed. Regretfully, his trust was not reciprocated and the cap was never returned to him.

SIXTEEN

Retirement

Stuart Surridge announced his retirement at the end of the 1956 season and the following article written by Kenneth Ritchie appeared in the magazine *Everybody's*:

For William Stuart Surridge it is the end of a career – what lies ahead for this dynamic cricketing captain?

'I shall be able to play more golf,' he says. 'Oh, for a spot of normal home life,' sighs his wife Betty from the Surridge home in Earlsfield. 'We'll be able to go away on holiday together' cries four-year-old Stuart Surridge junior. 'We have only had one holiday since we were married thirteen years ago,' says Betty. 'And that was late in September. It would never have occurred to me to suggest a holiday whilst cricket was being played!'

Betty Surridge has played the dual role of 'cricket widow' and 'ambassador's wife' ever since Stuart started his county on their record-breaking run. They met at a wartime dance at Upminster. Stuart readily forgave the pretty brunette the fact that her father had been a member of the Essex County Cricket Club for twenty years. And Betty, with her eyes wide open, embraced a life in which cricket was to take so dominant a place.

She soon learnt to keep her best china hidden away at the start of the cricket season. 'Stuart had his own way of getting into fielding trim before each season started,' explains Betty. 'He would throw a squash ball

Presentation box.

into odd corners of the kitchen and practice catching it from unexpected angles. It was sometimes hard on the crockery, but I always consoled myself with the thought that the Surrey bowlers would benefit!'

Stuart played in just one more first-class game after his retirement, when Surrey were invited to play two matches in Rhodesia in 1959 and Surridge lead the side in the first match. The match came down to the wire with the home team dismissing Surrey in the second innings for 107 with Mansell having match figures of 13-120. Despite a century by Barrington in the first innings and an excellent match by Lock, who took 11-120, Surrey were unable to force the win and lost by just two runs. Surridge bowled only four overs in the first innings.

He continued to play for Old Emanuel and also played in special matches raising money for charity. This included two matches in aid of the National Playing Fields Association, whose president was the

Duke of Edinburgh, a keen cricketer who played in these games. In 1957 the Duke of Edinburgh's team played the Duke of Norfolk's team at Arundel Castle. The other players in the team were: E.R.T. Holmes, A.B. Sellars, S.C. Griffith, B.A. Barnett, I. Craig, J.H. Parks Sr, J.M. Sims, James Langridge and G. Cox.

The following year the Duke of Edinburgh's team played against Lord Porchester's team at Highclere Park, Hampshire. This time other players in the team were: E.R.T. Holmes, New Zealanders J.R. Reid and W.R. Playne, D.C.S. Compton, W.J. Edrich, E.D.R. Eagar, C.H. Palmer, D.V.P. Wright and S.C. Griffith.

In 1961 Surridge captained a side that visited Bermuda. The rest of the side, of which all but three had experience of first-class cricket, were K. Cranston (vice-captain), K.C. Boles, G.P.S. Delisle, C.B.R. Fetherstonhaugh, J.C.L. Gover, T.W. Graveney, J.K. Hall, I.R. Lomax, M.P. Murray, W. Murray Wood, M.J. Osborne. A.C. Revill and J.K.E. Slack. Only Graveney had previously played cricket in Bermuda in 1953 and 1956. The team played twelve matches during their three-week stay, winning five and drawing the other seven. The highlight of the tour was the game against the Pick of Bermuda when Surridge's XI was forced to follow-on having been dismissed in their first innings for 113. However, they survived for a draw as Tom Graveney scored 205 not out in the second innings of 323/5. Surridge saved his best performance for the last match, again against Pick of Bermuda, when he took six successive wickets in less than an hour, including three in five balls. He had been handicapped for most of the tour because of a split finger restricting him to just 34 overs in total, during which he took a total of nine wickets at 11.55.

There are strong connections at the Oval with Emanuel School. The Surrey President of 2007, Vic Dodds and a past president, Derek Newton, both went to Emanuel. Vic Dodds was captain of the XI in 1962 and recalls:

Surridge brought an MCC team to play Emanuel School, MCC batted first and with Emanuel holding all their catches were dismissed for under 100. By 2 p.m. the school had won the game. Dodds approached Surridge and suggested they play another game as parents had arrived to

Portrait of Surridge which hangs in Long Room at the Oval.

watch their sons playing against MCC. Surridge's reply was 'You've won the game. I'm going home.'

On another occasion, Surridge turned up to play for Old Emanuel against Old Rutlishians just after scoring runs for Surrey Second XI. Asking what position he would be batting, the skipper told him no.4. The first three included his brother, Percy. Stuart was not well pleased, particularly as Old Emanuel declared at 240/2, at the fall of the second wicket. Stuart Surridge then went out to bowl, nicely fired up, and took 8-12.

A report in *The Cricketer* highlighted a match where Old Emanuel were set to score 83 runs in 54 minutes but with the batting of Surridge the target was achieved with 20 minutes to spare – his principal scoring strokes were nine fours and a six.

He was elected to the Surrey committee on giving up the captaincy and subsequently took over the chairmanship of the Cricket Sub-committee. He had the satisfaction of seeing yet another Championship win under the captaincy of Micky Stewart in 1971. He was president of the club in 1981 and during this period a portrait was painted of him and it now hangs in a prominent position in the long room at the Oval.

His involvement in the welfare of Surrey players, both past and present, is apparent by the comments made by Mark Peel in his biography of Ken Barrington entitled *England Expects – A Biography of Ken Barrington*:

> For the England tour to West Indies in 1980/81 because of economic considerations the role of Ken Barrington as assistant-manager was considered superfluous. This was not well received by the players and the press and substantial pressure was exerted on the authorities to change their decision.
>
> Surridge remembers the occasion. The Barringtons were staying at his home, and, returning from dinner, they found a note asking them to ring Lord's in the morning. Guessing the implications of the message, Surridge begged Barrington, his old friend, not to go, feeling that the pressure would be too severe. But Barrington, backed by his wife

'Tiger' Surridge.

Ann, was not to be deterred; he was overjoyed at his late inclusion and adamant about going. A standard medical check-up revealed nothing untoward, and he began to make the usual arrangements for his absence. A few weeks later he died from a massive heart attack in the West Indies following extensive political moves which threatened to cancel the tour.

Apart from his cricket, Stuart Surridge was a single handicap golfer. Naturally he was a long hitter and Alf Gover recalled partnering him in the annual County Cricketers' Golf Society match against the Professional Golfers when he constantly out-distanced the long ex-Ryder Cup golfers Alf Padgam and Alan Dailey off the tee. I always felt that had his first choice been golf and not cricket he would have become a top-class golfer. He was also a first class shot, being much in demand in the winter months in shoots all over the country.

He and his wife Betty gave many a party in their big Victorian Earlsfield house, and Stuart's welcome with a big happy smile and hand outstretched in greeting will long be remembered by all his friends from all over the world.

His son, Stuart Spicer Surridge known as 'Tiger' played for Surrey Second XI over a period of ten years from 1971–1980 and made his only first-class appearance against the Pakistani touring team in 1978. During that period he appeared in 39 matches, had 54 innings and scored 697 runs at 18.83. His highest score was an unbeaten 56 in the 1979 season. 'Tiger' was a wicketkeeper and took 64 catches and made 27 stumpings. At county level competition is always very fierce for wicketkeepers and at Surrey Jack Richards was the first-team keeper. He had offers to play for both Derbyshire and Middlesex but stayed loyal to Surrey, being very much influenced by his father. By that time he was heavily involved in the family business.

Although he had retired from cricket, Stuart continued to lead an active life, particularly where the family business was concerned, and it was on a visit to the factory in Glossop that he died on 13 April 1992. His widow, Betty, became the first lady to hold the office of president of any county cricket club when invited to accept the presidency of Surrey in 1997. To this day no other woman has been invited to be a president of any of the first-class counties.

In the article she wrote for the Surrey Yearbook she commented:

I was delighted and honoured to be invited by the club in March 1996 to be deputy president for the 1996 season, taking over as president in 1997. When Michael Soper asked me, on behalf of the club, I immediately accepted, not fully realising what it would entail. When I say that I did not realise what becoming president would entail, I suppose that I should have known from experience when I married Stuart I soon enough realised that once one marries or gets involved with cricket, one becomes part of the 'cricket family'. The only thing that had not dawned on me was that once one is part of that family, one is part of it for life.

From that fateful day, our house has always been populated with cricketers 'popping in for a quick drink', but more often than not staying all night. If walls could talk, the 'Earlsfield Arms', as it became known, would be able to recount many hundreds of cricketing stories and arguments from such great cricketers as Alf Gover, Peter May, the Bedsers, Kenny Barrington, Jim Laker, Micky Stewart and a host of others. I always remember also Stuart's great friendship with Billy Sutcliffe, who would often come and stay with us. Stuart always said that some of the toughest matches were against Yorkshire, but even though the matches were hard, he developed many great friendships with the Yorkshire players. In fact, Billy's father, the late great Herbert Sutcliffe, was a close friend of my father-in-law, and Billy first stayed in our house when he was only nine years old: long before my time.

It is interesting to recall the many great sportsmen, not just cricketers, who visited our house and our showroom in Borough High Street. The famous Australian cricketer Bill Brown, and his wife, stayed with me last year and we recalled the time their son, (Peter) was living in London and got married from our house. Stuart took Peter and his brother, the best man, to Moss Bros early in the morning of the wedding to get fitted up with morning suits, plus toppers, etc. This was a complete surprise to their parents, who didn't recognise their sons when they walked into the church. Barbara Brown still says to this day that they never looked so smart and knowing how casually most Australians dress, probably never will again.

When I think of some of the other amusing incidents that have happened over the years, one of the strangest must be that I somehow ended up on

Betty Surridge at The Ova l.

honeymoon with Alec Stewart's parents plus the whole Surrey team and several other wives also. Although Stuart was rather chauvinistic and never believed in women going on cricket tours, when I think of that happening, I think that perhaps he would quietly be rather proud of the great honour bestowed on me by the committee and members of the club.

After Stuart died, I was not quite sure how my relationship with Surrey would progress. As the wife of a famous cricketer who had passed away, it is always difficult to know what to do, and one always feels a bit of a 'spare part'. I think this is partially to do with the fact that, even though the wives have often been watching cricket for a long time, they are always insecure talking about it, and are worried that they might say the wrong thing. My own solution to this difficult problem is to avoid being drawn into conversation about the finer technical points of the game, and to carefully change the subject if it seems to be getting too technical. I know in discussions with other wives how difficult they find this situation but Surrey have always made us feel very much at home, and have always taken special care to invite widows along to functions at the Oval.

I was delighted to see the team having success last year and sincerely hope that we can continue to have more success in the current season. Much work has been going on behind the scenes to help us bring success back to the Oval, but I do not think it fair for me to single out any specific people. I just hope that we can all enjoy ourselves in 1997 and that I can contribute to this enjoyment in some small way.

Betty Surridge was one of the founder members of the Lady Taverners over twenty years ago when the Lord's Taverners decided to allow women into their organisation. Between the two organisations they have been responsible for raising large sums of money to support the game and, particularly, to help disabled children. The minibuses driving around the country proudly display the name of Lord's Taverners on their sides.

As mentioned in the opening chapter they are several memories of the Surridge family at the Oval where they have contributed so greatly to the history of Surrey County Cricket Club and all members happily recall the 'Five Glorious Years' at every appropriate opportunity.

What Makes a Successful Captain?

To win the County Championship in each of the five seasons of his captaincy is an achievement never likely to be equalled. Surridge was fortunate in having around him bowlers of the calibre of Alec Bedser, Laker, Lock and Loader and batsmen such as May and Barrington; so technical ability was always available. As has been shown so often in sport, mere ability is not enough and a leader is needed to direct such undoubted talents and instil a winning mentality. This was Stuart Surridge's achievement, and in those five years with Surridge at the helm, Surrey won 86 and lost only 20 of 139 Championship matches they played.

So what makes a successful captain? The modern description would be good 'man-management' and from all the comments made by his peers it is obvious that Stuart Surridge had the qualities of this in abundance. The ability to fashion Surrey's diverse and flowing abilities – and personalities – into one effective force proved to be the rare gift of a natural leader.

This chapter uses citations by Surridge's contemporaries who all give insight into why Surridge was so successful. The Surridge approach was dynamic – others have achieved this for a season or so, but Surridge did it for five years in a row and, what's more, he left the side as strong, if not stronger, than when he started. Fielding standards became almost unreal. Modern fielding is accepted as the last word in competence and athleticism but Surrey under Surridge must still be close to the ultimate

Stuart Surridge takes a catch watched by Jim Laker at slip and Arthur McIntyre.

yardstick. Without a helmet in sight, Surrey supported their unmatched attack with zeal and efficiency; many an unfortunate batsman, knowing his first half-mistake would be his last, must have thought the natural laws of justice were being roughly overthrown. Surridge had hands like buckets, a fearless disposition and he would never ask any fielder to do what he was not prepared to do himself.

He always led from the front. If he wanted a fielder very close to the bat for his spinners, he was the one to go into the danger area. He had 'grown up' in the cricketing world with many of his players and it is a measure of his character that he could lead with a firm hand and gain the respect of his team.

With such a formidable bowling line-up his chances to show his prowess with the ball were limited, and it was only when his main-line attack were away on Test duty that he could take the lead. He was still able to bowl himself in support of the stars, at fast-medium pace; bowling from his height with late away-swing he still managed to take over 500 wickets in his career. Indeed, for his exploits in 1953 he was listed by *Wisden* as one of their 'Five Cricketers of the Year', a singular honour. The citation was:

> Seldom does it fall to the lot of a cricketer to lead a side to the County Championship in his first year of captaincy as was the case in 1952 with Walter Stuart Surridge, of Surrey. Though not always free of criticism as regards tactics and the manner in which he handled the bowling, he brought to Surrey a spirit of consistent enterprise and aggression such as they had not known since the days of Percy Fender's captaincy twenty odd years previously. With the same players as comprised the team which finished sixth in the table a year before, Surrey, under his inspired command, swept to the county title with three matches in hand. Thus they amply justified Surridge's stated formula for successful captaincy: 'Attack all the time, whether batting, bowling or fielding.'
>
> In the nature of things the occasional upset occurred, but generally the harassing, chance-taking, opportunity-grasping policy of this popular, genial player, so rare in present-day English cricket, met with the reward it deserved. Successes came from the start, and even in the early weeks of the summer Surrey were freely spoken of as probable champions, with the name of Surridge and the virtue of his go-ahead methods inevitably coupled with such forecasets. Once again, as in the case of H.E. Dollery, who led Warwickshire to the title in 1951, was the value of spirited captaincy exemplified.

In February 1981 the Gloucestershire and Nottinghamshire cricketer, B.D. 'Bomber' Wells, wrote an article entitled 'Stuart Surridge, a natural leader' and sections of this article are quoted:

To some the name of Stuart Surridge may only be a cold printed fact in *Wisden Cricketers' Almanack*. So, too, is his incredible achievement of captaining Surrey to five consecutive Championship wins from 1952 to 1956.

What the entries cannot convey is what sort of man he was. The cynic will tell you that with players such as the Bedsers, Lock, Loader, Laker, May, Clark, Constable, Fletcher, McIntyre and company, any Tom, Dick or Harry could have been equally as successful. Yet Yorkshire were not exactly short of talent at that time. Nor were my county, Gloucestershire, yet we could not match Surridge's ability to raise everybody's game.

Another point which some carping criticism overlooks is that, while he had these star players, he also lost them for Test matches, MCC fixtures and other representative games. During a season he could lose four or five of them for at least seven to eight matches, yet he still worked the oracle without them. That was the measure of his leadership.

He seemed to have the knack of reading a player's character. He knew who to curse to get the best from them, and who to kid along to achieve the same results. To my mind he was a natural psychologist. He reminded me a great deal of Wilf Wooller. They were both big men, amateurs, bowling medium pace and both were gritty fighters with the bat. Each fielded at short leg and never asked anyone to do anything he would not do. They were two hard men.

Stuart's attitude to the game was not flamboyant, like, for example, Colin Ingleby-McKenzie's. He was more similar to a latter-day Brian Close. Many batsmen used to say they felt as though Stuart was *daring* them to play a shot when he breathed down their necks at short leg. Others thought he deliberately set his field close so that Lock and Laker dare not risk bowling off line. Of course, occasionally, they did stray ... And thereby hangs a tale.

Peter Rochford and I were batting. Now 'Rocky' was not renowned for his strength of shot and Laker's second or third ball pitched outside his leg stump. Rocky swept urgently at it and the ball flew straight at Stuart, striking him a fearsome blow on the forehead. Down he went but Locky, fielding next to him at short fine-leg, cried out 'catch it' as the ball shot into the air off his skipper's head. Whereupon wicketkeeper Arthur McIntyre did just that. Meanwhile Stuart had risen to his knees and was rubbing his head. 'Are you all right, Skip?' they asked. 'Did you catch it?' he replied, as if it was an everyday occurrence. When they confirmed the fact, he exclaimed 'Well bowled, Jim', while a rather bemused Rochy and myself made our way back to the pavilion.

As with all great leaders, he was a natural front man. He attacked whether he had Messrs Bedser & Co. or half the second team with him. Matches were rarely uneventful when he was around.

Peter May, who was to succeed Surridge as captain of Surrey, recalled in his book *A Game Enjoyed* that the main development in 1952 was, of course, the accession to the captaincy of Stuart Surridge:

He was simply a great and inspiring leader. To be successful, a captain needs to have good players and Stuart inherited them, but it was his outstanding achievement that he consistently got the best out of them. His enthusiasm was unlimited and infectious.

'It's no good being second,' he would say – and he always tried to win in the shortest possible time. He was lucky in having four world-class bowlers plus an off-spinner, Eric Bedser, who in any other county side would have done the double every season. Yet there were times when either one of the other fast bowlers was injured or when they were held up. Then Stuart would seize the ball himself.

'As for me,' he would say by way of field placing and we duly took our places. Then, with uncanny frequency, he would take an important wicket. He was already thirty-four in his first season of captaincy and I suppose that in the early part of a career interrupted by the war he had looked on himself, as others had, as a useful amateur to have in reserve and a fast-medium bowler above the average in second XI cricket.

I learned an enormous amount from him and not only about captaincy and cricket. In my young days I was a lively performer at the wheel of a red MG known as the 'fire engine'. Stuart Surridge taught me to drive safely, if still rather faster than seemed prudent to the chairman of selectors. Gubby Allen forbade me to drive at more than 50 miles an hour to Test matches.

In 1954, while playing in the last Test against Pakistan, I had missed another of Stuart's finest hours but it was graphically described to me.

On the last afternoon at Cheltenham the Surrey bowlers, although at full strength apart from Loader, were not making the progress to which Stuart was accustomed. Arthur Milton and Jack Crapp could be very obdurate. It began to rain with only four wickets taken and nothing in the sky suggested it was likely to stop. Stuart was in and out of the dressing room every few minutes examining the low cloud cover. Finally he came out and fairly glared in the direction from which the weather was coming. The rain stopped. Stuart lost no time in pointing this out to the umpires and hurried them out with the Surrey side hot on their heels. Of the six wickets remaining he took five himself, including one with a ball which unkind eyewitnesses say would have missed the leg stump by a foot if the batsmen's leg had not deflected it onto the wicket. When the last man was out and Surrey had won, Stuart relaxed and the rain belted down. I may not have been present to vouch for every detail of the story but it is a fair illustration of the drive and inspiration of Stuart's leadership.

Through those five years we had lost only two of the players who had launched us on the run – Laurie Fishlock and Jack Parker. They had been replaced by Micky Stewart and Ken Barrington. Micky, usually at square-short leg was a fearless close fielder in the same class as Stuart Surridge and Tony Lock. No helmets in those days. I doubt if it would have occurred to Micky to wear one if they had existed.

Yet the quality which I appreciate above all when I think back to the Surrey of the 1950s was the team spirit. This sounds like the usual platitude but it is more than that. I always had the feeling that if one of us made an exceptional individual contribution, its value to the side was uppermost in the mind of others. And, for that, one man was responsible, Stuart Surridge.

He was very much the players' champion, insisting that we all shared railway carriages and stayed at the same hotels, which had not previously been the custom. With his boundless energy, his drive, impatience, often unconventional approach and touch of irascibility, he was regarded with profound respect, trust and indeed affection. His style of captaincy was unusual, but it worked – and we all knew it did.

A previous very successful Surrey and England captain, Douglas Jardine, wrote an article for *Wisden* in 1957 entitled 'Stuart Surridge: Surrey's Inspiration'. Sections of the article are reproduced here:

Inspiration is the operative word. Exactly what inspiration may mean varies too much for exact definition or analysis. Leave it, therefore, that most people would claim to recognise it when they see it, and what is quite as important, everyone appreciates the difference between being at the sending or at the receiving end of inspiration.

Having got his inspiration, Mr Stuart Surridge was able not only to digest it, but to pass it on to each and every Surrey side from 1952 to 1956. In this, rather than in changing personnel, can be summed up the difference between the sides of 1948 to 1951.

To some extent Surridge's advent as leader may, from his own point of view, be considered to have been fortunately timed. It is no secret that during the years from 1948 to 1951 there was a very general conviction among players and members alike that there was present in the team, in good measure, all the ability and talent needed to win the County Championship. But the title continued to elude the county's grasp. The ability was never quite harnessed, or the talent fully and firmly exploited.

It is improbable that many recognised Surridge's inspiration for what it was. Few, however, could fail to appreciate his enthusiasm and the tautened determination springing naturally from it. The fielding had never been bad; no Oval crowd would tolerate that. But there was, nevertheless, a world of difference between the good workmanlike stuff served up before Surridge and the dynamic current with which he has charged it for the last five years. 'Don't drop a catch and you won't lose the match' is an old and tried adage. It would be no great exaggeration to say that the majority of catches missed by Surrey were chances only because they were made into 'possibles' by the fieldsmen. Surridge supplied the electricity close in on the off-side, while Lock did as much on the leg-side. To the unfortunate who had made nought in the first innings and was looking for a chance to 'get off the mark' in the second innings, the Surrey in-field must have offered anything but an alluring prospect.

Snapping up a chance at second slip.

Jim Laker in his book *A Spell from Laker* wrote:

> Over the years I have never wavered in my opinion that Stuart Surridge
> was the finest captain under whom I played. As I mentioned previously
> his appointment was by no means welcomed by all at the Oval, where
> the vast majority of captains had arrived via Oxford or Cambridge. Stuart
> was an Old Emanuel from Wandsworth who had played a fair amount of
> Surrey Second XI cricket, and his chief qualification in those days seemed
> to be the fact that he was a member of the unpaid ranks. The professional
> staff certainly did not expect him to be any better or worse than his
> predecessors but at least we knew him as a sincere and friendly colleague, a
> genuine amateur who would try to give all of us a fair crack of the whip.
>
> Possibly we did not appreciate immediately how much he respected
> the ability of the individuals he had inherited. As this became quickly

apparent to us our respect for Stuart as a leader and a competitor grew in leaps and bounds. There were those who were somewhat cynical of him as a cricketer, a view I could never share. On occasions he bowled really well. It is worth noting that in a relatively short first-class career he took no less than 506 wickets, which included 7-49 against a strong Lancashire side. Equipped, understandably, with the best piece of willow in the business (he makes bats) he cracked many useful runs in the lower order. Probably his unhappiest day was to fall thirteen runs short of a maiden century against Wilf Wooller's Glamorgan.

It was as a close catcher that he will probably be best remembered. Utterly fearless, he oozed confidence and firmly believed he could catch anything close to the wicket. He wanted and indeed expected a catch from every ball that came down: So often the good slip fielder, after dropping a couple of catches, hopes and prays that another will not quickly come his way. Not so Stuart Surridge. After a miss he desperately needed another chance to show the batsman how fortunate he had been. There is no doubt that this attitude of mind inspired Messrs Lock, Stewart and Barrington, and thanks to the skipper Surrey produced a magnificent quartet of close fieldsmen.

These alone were not the only qualities of a captain whose record surpasses anything before or since. He had the happy knack of bringing the best out of each individual player and was shrewd enough to appreciate that he could not handle, for instance, Tony Lock in the same manner as Alec Bedser. His approach to Peter Loader varied considerably from his attitude to me.

Mike Brearley, a captain of England in later years recalled in his book *The Art of Captaincy* that:

Certainly some players may react to robust leadership. Stuart Surridge was highly regarded as captain of the talented Surrey team in the early 1950s. His method of motivating Tony Lock was, I am told, to castigate, criticise and belittle him.

Winning meant everything to him and he frequently reminded all and sundry that 'you get nothing for coming second'. Consequently he always looked back with particular pride to 1955, when of the twenty-eight

County Championship matches, twenty-three were won, five lost and not a single game was drawn. Yorkshire, who had a wonderful side that year, finished runners-up and they, like us, broke the record for the number of points scored in a season. Only sixteen points separated the two of us.

Surridge's bold formula for success was keen and positive cricket. Restraint did not govern his game plan; in the words of Alec Bedser, he never departed from his philosophy of attack at all times, whether batting, bowling or fielding. One of the secrets of Surrey's eminence in the 1950s was the understanding built up during the apprentice years of those who commanded the Oval stage.

Raman Subba Row, the Croydon-born amateur and later an England representative, recalls the glow of delight at being invited by Surridge to join the Surrey ranks in 1953. He subscribed to the prevailing view of Surridge as a 'great leader of men' and immensely skilful in welding the mix of personalities in the team: 'No one was under any illusion as to what the score was when Stuart was in charge'. Surridge's discipline was often harsh and unnerving and he did not mince words with amateurs and professionals alike. Subba Row also points out that whatever the disagreements – and these could be explosive at times as in the best of families – Surridge never allowed resentment to simmer in the dressing room. The verbal sallies crackled like gunfire on occasions before the tempers cooled. Then, with the slate wiped clean, all was well. 'We can start afresh now,' said Surridge.

Raman Subba Row, held back in the order, was associated with Jim Laker in a thrilling finish against Sussex at Hove in 1954. On a perfect pitch a total of 1,279 runs were scored in the match. In the last innings Surrey were set a target of 239 and lost two quick wickets. In an attempt to catch up with the clock, the entire batting order was altered. 'Stewie said, "We'll have the right-handers in first,"' recalls Subba Row. 'I think he saw me as a slowcoach who would have held up the run-rate.' By the time he was at last permitted to bat at no.11, Laker had staunchly recorded a half-century, but nineteen runs were still required. Subba Row was quick enough to scamper two runs in the last over and Surrey hustled to victory in a tumult of excitement. The outrageous assault told a familiar tale. No one was allowed to sit on the splice with a win in the offing. Victory was achieved in two-and-a-half hours. In a day of helter-skelter cricket, 510 runs were scored in 123 overs.

Len Hutton once famously remarked in 1954, 'I do believe that the present Surrey side would have beaten the Yorkshire team of the 1930s.'

Doug Insole, as one of Surrey's opposing captains, says Surridge was unwaveringly confident in his own judgement: 'Stewie was a great character and some of his declarations were a little bizarre. He wanted to win matches in one day if possible. But he did have the standby of a second innings if matters went awry.'

Stuart Surridge, during Surrey's glorious years, once said: 'At the start my team was a little afraid to win the Championship. I had to give them a few kicks up the backside. But once they'd won it, they didn't want to lose it.' His sense of adventure and the exciting gambles caused consternation among county members as well as opponents. More often than not matches were completed before the end of the second day. 'We would pack our clubs and drive over to Wimbledon Park for a round of golf,' recalls Dave Fletcher. 'Our members got peeved because we were winning so quickly.'

The seventeen-year-old Tom Cartwright, playing in only his fifth first-class match came to the Oval in 1953 and played in the famous game which finished in one day. He recalled to Stephen Clarke in his biography:

Surrey's captain Stuart Surridge had revolutionised their fielding. He had put his best fielders close to the bat, even if they were bowlers, and that had allowed him to move the leg trap much closer to the batsmen. Stuart was a noisy, demonstrative man, very much a physical presence close to the wicket. Just handling the attack, moving the field, you were aware of him. It was very daunting, but it wasn't sledging. It was just a positive assertion that they were going to get you out, and this was how they were going to do it.

At 5.30 p.m., Tom was making his way to the middle in Warwickshire's second innings. He took guard on a pair and for a long time wondered if he could ever score a run:

It was very difficult to put a bat on Alec Bedser. I remember Arthur Mac standing up behind me, right up to the wicket, and leaping up to take the ball. The ball was pitching and going over my shoulder, and Eric at first slip was berating Alec for not bowling straight enough. And Laker at the other end was just as difficult. It was the first time I'd played against Surrey. I'd never seen any of them before. Going down to London, staying in the hotel, playing at the Oval, a big Saturday crowd, there was so much to take in. It was a bit overpowering.

Eventually, after what seemed a very long time, I decided to chance it. I swept Laker, top-edged it and it flew over Arthur Mac's head for three runs. Jim Laker trapped him lbw for nine. I'll never forget that game. County cricket on uncovered pitches was a great learning environment. I learned more in my time at the wicket in that game than I learned in any period of any other game.

An article in the *Daily Mail* on Saturday 27 August 1955 reflected:

Can Surridge and Surrey go one better next year and create a new record? Surridge is not yet certain whether to carry on. He told the crowd massed in front of the pavilion that 'it gets harder every year.' The present intention is to talk over his future with the committee. But there seems little doubt the club will be keen for Surridge to continue. For one thing Peter May, his successor, is almost sure to spend most of next summer helping England defend the 'Ashes.' Surridge, too, has created such a wonderful team spirit, and set such a standard of efficiency in fielding and catching, that Surrey will not willingly waste these priceless assets. This is no reflection on his successor, but team spirit has to be built up.

I cannot see in seasons immediately ahead either Surrey or Yorkshire relaxing their hold at the head of affairs. Both teams have brilliant cricketers and adequate reserves, but Surrey have the edge in attack. And, as Surridge commented: 'Individual performances often account for much, but once more a splendid team spirit has pulled us through. I see no reason why we should not hold the title again.

Many imagine that because Surrey's resources are so strong the team is capable of captaining themselves. I do not share that view, because

Surridge's enthusiasm and leadership are the reasons why Surrey remain at the top. Actually, the team is unbalanced. The batting is erratic and often fragile.

Alf Gover writing in the *Sunday Pictorial* on 26 August 1956 reported:

Stuart Surridge, Surrey's burly swashbuckling skipper, broke the news to me last night that this will be his last season as captain at the Oval. 'The decision had to be made some time' says thirty-nine-year-old Stuart. 'It's time I made way for a younger man. I've no regrets – cricket's been good to me.' Equally, skipper Surridge, the bold buccaneer who inspires his team by personal example, has been good for cricket.

Surrey will miss the dynamic leadership that steered them to four consecutive Championships and, barring miracles, a record five-in-a-row within the next few days. Now, however, Stuart feels the time has come to spend more time with his wife and four-year-old son, Stuart, junior. Somehow, this human dynamo has managed to fit in full-time cricket with family business interests that include two farms and a sports equipment firm.

Surridge brought this tremendous drive to Surrey cricket with results that shout for themselves. On the field he spares neither himself nor his side in the quest for victory. Mistakes, whether by Test stars or young colts, are not allowed to pass without scathing rebuke. I've heard rumours about his dominant personality and drive upsetting the players. Forget them. The players respect him as a born leader of men. Forget, too, those ill-founded whispers of a clash between Stuart and Peter May, England's skipper, who plays under his leadership. They compare notes. Often they differ on tactical moves, but Peter never disputes Surridge's authority as 'The Boss.' I discussed Stuart's captaincy with May during the current Test at the Oval. 'It's his will to win that has had so much to do with Surrey's success,' said Peter. 'He goes for victory from the gun. His enthusiasm is infectious. It gets into your bones. Since being with Surrey, I've found that my own will-to-win has become intensified. I'm sure the rest of the team has been affected the same way.

One of the most fascinating articles written about Surridge was by the famous writer, A.A. Thomson, and appeared in *Yorkshire Life Illustrated* in November 1954:

I want to praise the captain of the county that has won the Championship for the last three years in succession; a leader of forceful character and his achievement. And, you know, it is practically impossible for a Yorkshireman to praise a captain without comparing him with Brian Sellers. Our feeling is that Brian Sellers is the touchstone. In 1932 he took over from that excellent player and skipper, Frank Greenwood, and between then and 1946, the first season after the war, led his team to victory in seven seasons out of nine. Nobody else has done anything quite like that.

That stout-hearted Lancastrian, Leonard Green, led his county to the top three times in a row in the exciting years of 1926–28 and, after that, it was not long before the White Rose took over from the Red. After three Championships, Green retired and so he achieved a hundred per cent record of victory. With Surrey's triumph in the wet and sombre season that has passed, both Sellers and green have a rival.

On the stage bursts the big burly figure of Stuart Surridge, like Sellers a forceful personality and a daring fielder close to the wicket. To the bulk of an amiable buffalo he adds the agility of a jaguar. I once heard an admirer at the Oval say of his slip catches: 'He don't catch 'em; he eats 'em!'

What kind of fellow then, is this leader in a hat-trick of victories? First, he is a big man, both in body and spirit. He is a big man; was a big boy, and, I should imagine, must have been a big baby. At any rate he was playing at school at the age of eight. His family had been for more than one generation manufacturers of bats and other cricket equipment. In winter he works hard at this business, besides giving an eye to two farms, where grow the willows which the family firm shapes into bats. He progressed in his bustling way through the various grades of cricket at his school, Emanuel, which is an excellent cricketing school, anyway. First he was in the under-fourteens, then the colts, then in the First XI, which he captained in his last year at school, when he was seventeen.

It is typical of him that until he was fifteen he was a wicketkeeper. Why? 'They wanted a wicket-keeper.' You may have seen him at slip

Surridge hits lustily to
leg in trademark style.

or short leg suddenly (and laterally) hurl his fourteen-and-a-half stone, taking a somersault and a flying ball at the same instant. Maybe he was born with that jet-propelled jump; maybe he learnt it keeping wicket. Then in the last couple of school seasons he became a fast bowler. ('Oh, well, they *wanted* a fast bowler…')

He was born a volunteer for energetic jobs. I can well imagine him modestly receiving a medal for gallantry and murmuring: 'Oh, well, they *wanted* a chap for stopping runaway trams…' He became a schoolboy member of the Surrey club when he was twelve and that put him in a position to see something worth watching, an eleven captained by P.G.H. Fender, and headed in the batting order by Sir Jack Hobbs and Andy Sandham, the only serious rivals as a pair to our own Holmes and Sutcliffe. And young Surridge did something better than watching: he became a pupil at the Easter classes at the Oval, which were looked after that cheerful Surrey stalwart, Alan Peach, who had never had sufficient praise for his sterling work as batsman, bowler, fielder and coach. He learned a lot from Peach and in the winter he learned a lot more from the school run by Sandham and Gover.

The coaching he received from Gover was of the utmost value to the budding attacker, for Gover is one of the best fast bowlers Surrey, or any other county, ever had. His record would have been much better if he had had better support from the slip fielders of his period. There is a tale (no doubt apocryphal) that Gover was once having a drink with his fellow players after a particularly unhappy afternoon of lapses in the slips. 'Well, so long, Alf', said one of the leading offenders, 'I've got to catch a train.' 'So long,' said Gover cheerfully. 'Hope you have better luck… with the train.' Under Gover's tuition Surridge's bowling action was greatly improved and was already on its way to becoming the bustling businesslike affair that it is today.

In 1952 he was appointed captain and it was no coincidence that Surrey had the best season they had had for nearly forty years. Actually they had tied with Lancashire at the top of the table two years before but they had not won the Championship outright since 1914. The *Wisden* of the time had no doubt whatever about the main cause of this victory. 'One reason for Surrey's tremendous advance was the confident assurance of all the players in their own abilities, and for that happy frame of mind they had to thank Surridge…' He believed in attacking all along the line and going all out for twelve points from the first ball sent down. Time and again in that exciting season Surrey would knock off the runs in the fourth innings on a dusty wicket. Boldness was their friend, and only courage and confidence pulled them through. Typical of this kind of game was the one against Kent at the Oval, where Surrey were set 192 to win in 90 minutes. With an hour to go, they still needed 128, and wickets kept falling. Each batsman hurried to the crease and when Surridge made the winning hit – it *would* be Surridge – the clock's minute hand was dickering on half-past six and the Oval crowd were on their feet and yelling their heads off.

In that season, too, Surridge set up a Surrey record by taking 58 catches in a season. I cannot think offhand of any player other than a wicketkeeper, who has done better than that. In the three Championship seasons he has held nearly 150, and from what I have seen, he 'made' a large number of them, which would not have been catches at all to a less acrobatic fieldsman.

In 1953 the record was not quite so good, only thirteen victories being won instead of twenty, and early in 1954, the wettest of seasons, Surrey were robbed of win after win by the malevolent caprice of the weather. Yorkshire were well ahead and then, nine games from the end of the season, Surrey flung themselves into a terrific spurt. Yorkshire, alas, wavered, and Surrey ran out with seven wins out of those last nine games.

Yorkshiremen may take a little wry comfort from claiming that Surrey took a leaf out of their own book. In Yorkshire's greatest days (and they are coming back again) they won by having three bowlers around the top of the averages – Surrey had four – and by winning their vital matches in two days. Asked how it was done, Surridge said it was teamwork. Of course it was teamwork, but if anyone thinks that the splendid thing called teamwork can happen without leadership, he thinks something extremely foolish. Yorkshire's greatest days, I say, are coming again, but, if only Stuart Surridge had been born in Cleckheaton, Liversedge or Heckmondwike, they might have come sooner.

Another famous writer of the time, John Arlott wrote in his *Review of Surrey* in 1954:

The expression 'worthy champions' has been used so often as to have lost much of its meaning. Let us say of Surrey that, to complete their third consecutive Championship win in 1954, they produced that electric quality which could mark the difference between the best side in the country and Championship *winners*.

Last season Yorkshire were, arguably and man-for-man, a better side than Surrey. By the start of the run-in, at the beginning of August, Derbyshire, with their shrewd power of winning matches on a slim allowance of runs, looked likelier winners.

At that stage of the rain-plundered summer only one man in England believed that Surrey would win the Championship. He was their captain, Stuart Surridge. He set out to come from behind and beat not only the opposing counties, but the weather as well. And he could not rely on three days to a match. Of the last ten games, nine were won – five of them in two days. The chocolate caps marked cricket as killing as that of any of the Yorkshire juggernauts of the past.

Say, if you like, that Laker and Lock did it. Certainly they have proved greater bowlers for Surrey than for England. Or say, with as much accuracy, that Stuart Surridge lifts them to their greatest heights by his determined captaincy.

Mark him well, this man Surridge. He is not so young as his manner; for all his drive and enthusiasm he was rising thirty-five when he came into the Surrey captaincy in 1952. If some of the critics had had their way he would have been dropped a couple of years ago. But without him I doubt if Surrey would now be champions.

There are, to be sure, better players by strictly technical standards, but none who so combine ordinary gifts with determination. He is an 'agricultural' type of batsman, but it is probably true to say that no player with so low a batting average has made so many of his runs with such match-winning effect. As a fieldsman he will plant himself suicidally close to the bat, *demanding* catches and taking them plentifully – only six players apart from wicket-keepers beat his thirty-eight catches last season. Bustlingly, alert, sandy-haired, his face pink and freckled, and with a grin of infectious breadth, Stuart Surridge is a friendly man. At the Oval, where the captain is the sole team-selector, he has gone out of his way to encourage the tryer, the good player out of form. How much longer will he captain Surrey? His reply is the one you would expect: 'I'll play as long as I'm fit.' No cricketer in the country devotes himself more slavishly to keeping fit; is capable of clearer self-criticism.

I would not call Peter May a brilliant captain, but he is one of cricket's most kindly and courteous personalities. Like Stuart Surridge, he is a 'pure' amateur. He plays the game with genuine devotion – almost love – and, in developing in to the first major Test batsmen produced by our post-war play, he has also given us the romantic picture of the natural games player.

As he reached his final season an article appeared in *The Cricketer* written by the Australian bowler and writer, W.J. O'Reilly entitled 'An Appreciation of Stuart Surridge'. He compared his cricketing skills with A.C. MacLaren who led Lancashire to two County Championship titles at the start of the twentieth century. He stated:

But no one in his right senses would class Surridge with MacLaren; least so Surridge himself. What has he that MacLaren lacked? One can certainly name a number of things that Surridge lacks, of what are considered essentials in a good captain. It is generally accepted that the captain should be first of all, worth his place as a player. In 1955 Surrey's captain, in 37 innings scored 330 runs; averaged 10, with a highest score of 33. Bowling figures in twenty-nine matches were 26 wickets at 30 runs each. 311 overs were bowled, approximate average five per innings. Nothing to boast about there! But 56 catches, third highest among fieldsmen, must have been serviceable.

Still, one is not chosen in county cricket for fielding alone. Plainly, his merit must lie in his captaincy. A captain should inspire. Surridge inspires every player in his team. The impression each one gives is that only his best is good enough for Surrey – and Surridge. In 1952 Surridge inherited a group of fine cricket individuals. He welded them into a team; galvanised them with his keen enthusiasm, geniality, and sporting disposition; then showed them how to win an honour denied them for nearly forty years. And now they seem to have made a habit of it! A 'successful' captain, both on and off the field, in his own characteristic way; and a modest one. A worthy captain of a worthy team.

Don Mosey writing in his book *Laker: Portrait of a Legend* commented:

Salvation, at least for Laker's peace of mind, came in the burly form of Surridge. Here was a man very much to Jim Laker's liking: He will go down in the record books as a fairly ordinary cricketer, though in fairness his performances were always a little bit better than he was given credit for. But it was as a captain, a leader of men, that he was one of the most dynamic characters ever to set foot on a cricket field. He did not believe it was possible for Surrey to lose a match. As a result, he made a few mistakes, but not very many. He was also the greatest retriever of lost causes I have ever known. And he had the inborn knack of knowing how to handle individuals. One has to remember that that side, which eventually contained ten Test cricketers, included some very different temperaments and personalities. All in all, he was a very popular guy, even in the professionals' dressing room.

Perhaps the most remarkable revelation to emerge from a long conversation with Stuart Surridge was that when Jim took all ten Australian wickets for Surrey in 1956, 'he only really turned one ball'. And just how did that come about?

Well, it was a beautiful wicket. Simply, he kidded them. He could do it all, off the pitch, through the air. He could turn it when he wanted to. But he could do it all, you see. I might mention that some people used to talk a load of rubbish about the Oval wickets. I never asked the groundsman to produce a particular kind of wicket; we played on what he produced and I think you'll find the seamers actually took more wickets than Laker and Lock.

Ken Barrington was quoted in the *Daily Mail* on 25 May 1971:

Stuart Surridge did a wonderful job in getting the best out of those great spin-twins Jim Laker and Tony Lock in Surrey's great years of triumph. They had to be handled differently. Jim needed calm treatment, but with Tony Lock, Surridge used the kind of language that would make John Snow's father, the vicar of Bognor Regis, blush.

One aspect of the captaincy imposed on Stuart Surridge that is not generally known is that Surrey operated a Talent Bonus Money scheme for the professionals on the staff; the amount of bonus being decided by a points system calculated by the captain. In 1952 the total bonuses amounted to £600 rising to £900 in 1956. The most successful players received between £60 and £80 per season from this 'pool' but in 1956 Tony Lock topped the payout with £100. All these figures are recorded in the Minutes of the Surrey CCC Cricket Sub-committee.

Statistics

First-class Career of Stuart Surridge

Season by Season

	M	I	NO	HS	Runs	Ave	Ct	Overs	M	Runs	W	Ave	BB
1939	1	1	0	20	20	20.00	1	36.0	4	100	8	12.50	5-41
1947	6	8	1	28	116	16.57	4	140.4	19	445	10	44.50	3-55
1948	24	38	7	33*	441	14.22	16	670.3	153	1,830	64	28.59	7-82
1949	21	28	2	41*	300	11.53	27	548.5	98	1,813	68	26.66	6-49
1950	32	46	5	55	438	10.68	38	922.1	202	2,469	79	31.25	6-55
1951	26	31	1	87	351	11.70	33	658.1	144	1,658	54	30.70	7-49
1952	32	34	3	59	541	17.45	58	770.1	165	1,967	78	25.21	7-80
1953	32	37	2	53	433	12.37	48	615.5	118	1,813	56	32.37	5-46
1954	31	31	2	54	341	11.75	39	423.3	82	1,101	46	23.93	6-31
1955	29	36	4	33	330	10.31	56	311.4	73	783	26	30.11	6-56
1956	32	41	6	70*	557	15.91	54	285.0	63	634	17	37.29	5-57
1959/60	1	2	0	12	14	7.00	2	4.0	1	10	0		
Total	267	333	33	87	3,882	12.94	376	5,386.3	1,122	14,623	506	28.89	7-49

For each team

	M	I	NO	HS	Runs	Ave	Ct	Overs	M	Runs	W	Ave	BB
Surrey	254	316	32	87	3,697	13.01	361	5,102.3	1,081	13,753	464	29.64	7-49
Surrey XI	1	1	0	0	0	0	0	32.0	6	92	7	13.14	4-29
Gentlemen	3	2	0	2	3	1.50	1	57.0	3	241	6	40.16	2-30
MCC	3	5	0	27	66	13.20	1	45.0	12	104	5	20.80	3-22

Minor Counties	1	1	0	20	20	20.00	1	36.0	4	100	8	12.50	5-41
Over 32	1	2	0	18	18	9.00	1	16.0	4	48	1	48.00	1-3
S. of England	3	5	1	26	58	14.50	10	76.0	9	240	14	17.14	7-82
T.N. Pearce's XI	1	1	0	20	20	20.00	1	22.0	3	45	1	45.00	1-31
Total	267	333	33	87	3,882	12.94	376	5,386.3	11,221	14,623	506	28.89	7-49

Batting

Analysis of Innings Scores				Methods of Dismissal		
Score	No. of Times	Not Out		Bowled	127	(42.3 per cent)
0	57	0		Caught	146	(48.7 per cent)
1–9	132	10		lbw	13	(4.3 per cent)
10–19	80	9		Stumped	8	(2.7 per cent)
20–29	35	4		Run Out	6	(2.0 per cent)
30–39	15	5		Total	300	
40–49	4	3				
50–59	8	1				
60–69	0	0				
70–79	1	1				
80–89	1	0				
Total	333	33				

He was dismissed for no score in both innings [a pair] on three occasions:

1948 *v.* Middlesex at Lord's dismissed by D.C.S. Compton in both innings

1949 *v.* Worcestershire at Worcester dismissed by R.O. Jenkins in both innings

1950 *v.* Essex at the Oval dismissed by R. Smith in both innings

Bowlers who took his wicket most often:

11   J.H. Wardle (Yorkshire)

9   C. Cook (Gloucestershire)

8   M.J. Hilton (Lancashire/MCC)

6   R. Tattersall (Lancashire), F.J. Titmus (Middlesex)

5   R. Smith (Essex)

Bowling
How Wickets Taken

Bowled	146	(28.8 per cent)
Caught	298	(58.9 per cent)
lbw	59	(11.7 per cent)
Stumped	3	(0.6 per cent)
Total	506	

Batsmen most frequently dismissed:

7   F.C.Gardner (Warwickshire)

6   E.Davies (Glamorgan) T.C.Dodds (Essex), G.M. Emmett (Gloucestershire), D.M.Young (Gloucestershire/MCC)

5   W.J. Edrich (Middlesex), W.Place (Lancashire), J.D.B.Robertson (Middlesex), H.W. Stephenson (Somerset), C.Washbrook (Lancashire)

Most catches taken off his bowling:

Career			In a Season	
77	A.J.W. McIntyre	Wicketkeeper	14	A.J.W. McIntyre
32	G.A.R. Lock	Fielder	8	J.F. Parker
21	A.V. Bedser		7	G.A.R. Lock
18	E.A. Bedser		6	A.V. Bedser, G.A.R. Lock
17	J.C. Laker			
17	J.F. Parker			
13	B. Constable			
12	W.S. Surridge			
11	D.G.W. Fletcher			

Catching
In his career Surridge took 376 catches fielding in close positions. The bowlers off whom he took most catches were:

108 J.C. Laker

79   G.A.R. Lock

69   A.V. Bedser

43   E.A. Bedser
19   P.J. Loader

Career Highlights for Surrey:

First 5 wickets in an innings: 25.5-8-50-5 *v.* Warwickshire at the Oval, 19 June 1948

First half century: 55 *v.* Sussex at Hastings, 9 August 1950

Last Match for Surrey in England: *v.* Rest of England at the Oval, 8 September 1956

Last Match for Surrey: *v.* Rhodesia, Salisbury (now Harare), 10 October 1969

Best bowling in an innings: 7-49 *v.* Lancashire at the Oval, 5 May 1951

Best bowling in a match: 10-117 *v.* Glamorgan at the Oval, 19 May 1951

Most overs bowled in an innings: 43.4 *v.* Glamorgan at the Oval, 1 June 1955

Most overs bowled in a match: 61.4 *v.* Glamorgan at the Oval, 1 June 1955

Most runs conceded in an innings: 123 v. Australians at the Oval, 1 July 1948

Most runs conceded in a match: 166 *v.* Australians at the Oval, 1 July 1948

Most catches in an innings: 5 *v.* Lancashire at the Oval, 25 May 1955

Most catches in a match: 7 *v.* Leicestershire at the Oval, 6 July 1955

When he took 51 catches for Surrey in 1952 it was the most ever held in a season by one player for Surrey. In 1955 he bettered his own record with 55 catches.

This record was subsequently broken by M.J.Stewart in 1967 who took 77 catches.

Bibliography

Barty-King, H., *Quilt Winders and Pod Shavers*, Macdonald and James, 1979

Brearley, M., *The Art of Captaincy*, Guild Publishing, 1985

Chalke, S., *At the Heart of English Cricket – The Life and Memories of Geoffrey Howard*, Fairfield Books, 2001

Chalke, S., *Tom Cartwright – The Flame Still Burns*, Fairfield Books 2007

Gover, A., *The Long Run*, Penguin Group, 1991

Hignell, A., *Rain Stops Play*, Frank Cass Publishers, 2002

Hill, A., *The Bedsers – Twinning Triumphs*, Mainstream Publishing, 2001

Laker, J., *A Spell from Laker*, Hamlyn Publishing, 1979

Lemmon, D., *Changing Seasons*, Andre Deutsch, 1997

Lodge, J., *Surrey County Cricket Club: 100 Greats*, Tempus Publishing, 2003

Lodge, J., *Into the Second Century*, Tempus Publishing, 2004

Lodge, J., *Surrey County Cricket Club, Fifty Classic Matches*, Tempus Publishing, 2006

Marshall, *From Willow to Wicket*, 'The Sportsman', 1911

May, P., *A Game Enjoyed*, Stanley Paul & Co. Ltd, 1985

Miller, D., *Allan Watkins – A True All-Rounder*, Association of Cricket Statisticians and Historians, 2007

Morgan, G.H., *Forgotten Thameside*, Letchworth Printers, 1966

Mortimore, G., *The Longest Night*, Weidenfeld & Nicolson, 2005

Mosey, D., *Laker – Portrait of a Legend*, Queen Anne Press, 1989

Peel, M., *England Expects – Biography of Ken Barrington,* The Kingswood Press, 1992

Ramsey, W.G. [Ed.], *The Blitz, Then and Now, Vol. 2,* Battle of Britain Prints International Ltd, 1998

Ross, G., *A History of County Cricket – Surrey*, 1971

Ross, G., *The Surrey Story*, Stanley Paul, 1957

Scovell, B., *Ken Barrington – A Tribute,* Harrap Ltd, 1982

Steer, D., *Cricket – The Golden Age*, Octopus Publishing, 2003

Watling, D.A., *The Life and Times of the Cricket Bat Willow*, Hassan Mughal, 1998

Various editions of:
Surrey CCC Yearbooks
The Cricketer
Wisden Cricketers Almanacks

Index

Moss, A.E. 102, 126
Moss Bros. 160
Mucking, Essex 23, 24, 29
Murray, M.P. 155
Myers, E.B. 150

National Playing Fields
    Association 154
Newington Causeway,
    London SE1 18
Newton, D. 155
Nicholls, R.B.136
Nixon, Thomas 18, 21, 22
Norfolk, Duke of 155
North, R.E. & Co. 71
Northampton 116, 126, 136
Northamptonshire CCC
    42, 56, 61, 84, 91, 92,
    98, 103, 108, 109, 116,
    122, 127, 135, 140
Nottinghamshire CCC 36,
    40, 84, 89, 97, 101, 109,
    111, 118, 120, 125, 135,
    136, 142, 151, 165
Nutter, A.E. 42

Old Emanuel CC 12, 14,
    27, 35, 154, 157, 170
Old Trafford, 40, 94, 97,
    109, 117, 125, 145
Oldfield, N. 56
O'Reilly, W.J. 180
Old Rutlishians 158
Osborne, M.J. 155
Oxford University CC 27

Page, J.C.T. 140
Palmer, C.H.43, 61, 92,
    102, 119, 120, 122, 123,
    137, 155
Parker, J.F. 40, 78, 79, 80,
    81, 83, 87, 88, 89, 90, 91,
    92, 93, 131, 168
Parkhouse, W.G.A. 103,
    120, 124
Parkin, C.H. 61, 65
Parks, J.H. 155
Parks, J.M. 88, 127, 142
Parsons Green CC 15
Peach, H.A. 'Alan' 13, 14,
    25, 26, 178
Peebles, I.A.R. 63
Peel, Mark 157
Pettiford, J. 123

Phebey, A.H. 110
Pierpoint, F.G. 25, 27
Place, W. 35, 88, 185
Playle, W.R. 155
Pontypridd 108
Poole, C.J. 101, 136
Porchester, Lord 155
Portsmouth 137
Potter, G. 140
Pratt, D.E. 79, 142
Pratt, R.E.C. 79, 123, 128,
    135, 145
Preston, Hubert 63
Preston, K.C. 42, 121
Preston, Norman 59, 61,
    64
Price, W.F.F. 87
Pritchard, T.L. 99

Ranjitsinhji, K.R., Rajah
    of Patiala 20
Rayment, A.W.H. 104
Redman, J. 40
Reid, J.R. 155
Rest of England, The 116,
    186
Revill, A.C. 89, 155
Rhodes, H.J. 89, 135
Rhodesia 154, 186
Richards, C.J. 159
Ritchie, Kenneth 153
Robertson, J.D.B. 185
Rochford, P. 166
Robins, R.W.V. 48
Rockingham Street,
    London SE1 17, 18
Roehampton CC 26, 27
Roehampton Vale 23
Rogers, N.H.128
Root, C.F. 60
Ross, Gordon 105
Rowe, E.J. 101
Rugby School 18
Rushby, T. 150
Rushden 84
Russell Hill, Purley 22

Sainsbury, P.J. 128, 138
Sandham, A. 13, 14, 94,
    177, 178
Sayers, Bill 69
SDL Group 74
Sellers, A.B. 52, 61, 115, 130
Shackleton, D. 100, 138

Shaw, A. 114
Shepherd, D.J. 135
Sheppard, D.S. 61, 82, 98
Simmons, Fred 68
Simpson, R.T. 101, 111, 120
Sims, J.M. 155
Slack, J.K.E. 155
Smales, K. 135
Smith, D.V. 137
Smith, E. 128, 135
Smith, J.W.R. 141
Smith, R. 40, 184, 185
Smith, T.P.B. 40, 110, 121
Smith, W.C. 'Razor' 20, 150
Smithson, G.A. 102, 122,
    137
Snow, Rev. 182
Somerset CCC 40, 86, 95,
    97, 109, 119, 126, 137
Soper, Michael 160
South, The 39, 92
South Africans 43, 57, 117
Southampton 91, 103
Spicer, Alfred 29
Spooner, R.T. 108
Statham, J.B. 88, 113, 120
Stephenson, H.W. 185
Stewart, M.J.66, 68, 78,
    79, 80, 107, 111, 117,
    119, 123, 124, 125, 126,
    127, 128, 133, 137, 138,
    141, 142, 144, 145, 146,
    157, 160, 161, 168, 171
Stocks, F.W. 40, 136
Strudwick, H. 14,150
Subba Row, R. 78, 79, 93,
    95, 100, 101, 102, 103,
    104, 108, 109, 112, 122,
    172
Surrey Club & Ground
    CC 26
Surrey Music Hall 31
Surridge, Beatrice (Aunt)
    17, 22
Surridge, Betty (wife)
    29, 52, 73, 75, 153, 159,
    162
Surridge, Frederick (uncle)
    17, 23, 67
Surridge, Percival(father)12,
    17, 22, 25/26, 31, 67
Surridge, Percival Stuart
    (grandfather)
    11, 11, 12, 17-24